Abstract

The Applicability of Systems Thinking to Modern Entrepreneurs

by

Richard Holzmuller

MBA, National American University, 2009

BS, National American University, 2006

AAS, Community College of the Air Force, 2001

Doctoral Study Proposal Submitted in Partial Fulfillment

of the Requirements for the Degree of

Doctor of Business Administration

Walden University

December 2015

ISBN: 0-9993462-0-2

ISBN-13: 978-0-9993462-0-4

Abstract

The abstract is written after the doctoral study is completed. I submitted sections 1 and 2 of my doctoral study proposal December 2015, to my mentor, for approval. My mentor rejected my proposal, so I did not complete this study. Since I was not allowed to conduct the research I proposed in this study, I have no findings of my research to present or discuss in section 3, so there is no section 3. My mentor rejected my work, mostly because I use passive voice in my writing. The good things are: my form and style are good, there are no major gaps in concepts or design, and my writing passed plagiarism checks. Although I did not complete this doctoral study, I still think readers can glean benefits from it.

The Applicability of Systems Thinking to Modern Entrepreneurs

by

Richard Holzmuller

MBA, National American University, 2009

BS, National American University, 2006

AAS, Community College of the Air Force, 2001

Doctoral Study Proposal Submitted in Partial Fulfillment

of the Requirements for the Degree of

Doctor of Business Administration

Walden University

December 2015

Dedication

This book is dedicated to my mother; without her encouragement, I would not have even completed my Associate Degree.

Acknowledgments

I had three mentors/doctoral study committee chair people over the course of three years. My first mentor wanted to work with me, but then my second chairperson rejected my proposal. My second mentor was confused about my use of the word sustainability, and rejected my work because he did not think it was ready for the next stage. My third mentor rejected my proposal, mostly because of my use of passive voice. There were a few more rejections spattered amongst my mentors and second chairperson over those three years; with each rejection, I took it as a challenge to do better. After I dropped out of the doctoral study program, my third mentor said he said he was interested to co-author this book with me. By chance, I met a former Walden University professor who also reviewed and approved of this work. The comments from my former mentor and the former professor I met, reaffirmed my confidence in my work, and substantiated my decision to publish this doctoral study proposal.

Table of Contents

Section 1: Foundation of the Study

Some companies are not sustainable by design. Innovative leaders that recognize this problem make significant changes as a means to becoming sustainable. There is a vast amount of literature about sustainability and sustainability is a familiar topic in most media (Hinz, 2012); however, sustainability is still not well known. Sustainability is not well known because it is not the primary focus of most entrepreneurs. Most entrepreneurs are primarily concerned about making a profit (Wood, 2014). Later, when there is a need, business owners often attempt to transition their systems to something they perceive to be more sustainable than their current organizational practices (Hinz, 2012). Because sustainability is not well known, corporate leaders sometimes poorly execute a process to accomplish a sustainability objective, and consequently garner undesired results (Eccles & Serafeim, 2013). Leading-edge entrepreneurs see the value of systems thinking before they even begin development of their business, learn to identify systems intricacies, and continue to employ useful systems concepts to guide their decision-making process. This study will be about entrepreneurs that consciously consider systems from inception to execution. Research goals are to uncover why entrepreneurs start businesses with systems as a primary consideration, and how entrepreneurs continue to use systems thinking to guide their decision-making processes to generate desired results. The culmination of this work may provide a new business case for sustainability, as well as tactics and strategies for future entrepreneurs and managers that wish to incorporate systems thinking into their decision-making processes.

Background of the Problem

Some managers have not yet articulated their business case for sustainability; and, some managers may not understand why they need a business case for sustainability (Eccles & Serafeim, 2013). Confusion and misunderstanding regarding sustainability are often not immediately apparent, and, managers usually have time to develop solutions before problems become unmanageable (Ciemleja & Lace, 2011). However, when there is a lack of information or misinformation, managers make poor decisions, and a manageable problem may quickly become unsustainable. As an act of desperation, business leaders often make drastic changes to their business models to resolve the problem that is only an effect of their dysfunctional system (Li & Lin, 2011).

There have been several case studies of corporate leaders that have successfully transitioned their systems to include improved sustainability practices (Holliday, 2010; Amodeo, 2005; Mehalik, 2001). Butler's (2004) case study explained leveraging sustainability innovatively, and Johnson's (1996) comparative case study compared companies with sustainability practices and firms without sustainability practices. However, there may not be any information in the literature about leaders that had the foresight to include sustainability elements in the development of their organizational structure. Entrepreneurs that include sustainability in their business models have a business case for sustainability, and understand why sustainability is important to them. Entrepreneurs that are not confused by sustainability concepts may profitably incorporate sustainable functions, and adeptly identify weaknesses in their systems. The problem statement that follows provides clarity on the direction of research for this proposal.

Problem Statement

Globally, 63% of chief executive officers that profited from sustainability had changed their business model to incorporate sustainability (Kiron, Kruschwitz, Reeves, & Goh, 2013). 20% of global business leaders that employed a sustainability strategy without a business case for sustainability decreased their profits (Eccles & Serafeim, 2013). International business leaders that see the value of sustainability actively advance measures to operate sustainably (James, 2013). The general business problem is international business leaders that implement sustainable practices without a clear business case may not profit from those initiatives. There is literature about business leaders that have successfully transitioned to improved sustainability (Holliday, 2010; Amodeo, 2005; Mehalik, 2001). There is no literature regarding entrepreneurs that developed a business case for sustainability before they started their businesses. The specific business problem is international business managers do not establish a business case for sustainability before they incorporate sustainability.

Purpose Statement

The purpose of this qualitative single case study is to learn why international business managers have a business case for sustainability before they incorporate sustainability. The qualitative method and single case study design provide rich context for exploration of one company in detail (Reynolds, 2014). The targeted population is a consulting firm comprised of 59 experienced international product development professionals based on the East Coast of the United States. The industry leaders of the private organization help entrepreneurs develop their natural products ideas at every phase; from conception, to the retail outlet. Established in 2012, the natural products mavens have already fostered the development of 33 new brands. The consultants of the organization subscribe to the guiding principles of people-planet-profit-purpose as they serve their clients. The values-driven services the experts provide suggests the leaders understand why international business managers establish a business case for sustainability before they incorporate sustainability. Methods of inquiry include individual semi-structured interviews with 20 members of the management team (Reynolds, 2014). This study may yield new information that can benefit social change scholars and practitioners that desire to develop or improve their business case for sustainability knowledge, tactics, or strategy.

Nature of the Study

The qualitative method and case study design will be used to explore the complexities of why international business managers develop a business case for sustainability before they incorporate sustainability. The qualitative model is appropriate for this research study to explore and richly describe the contemporary phenomenon of sustainability from the viewpoint of the participants (Reynolds, 2014). Qualitative research is necessary to build inductively, an understanding of why international business managers develop a business case before implementing sustainable elements (Hinz, 2012). Contrastingly, the quantitative design is primarily useful for researchers to test a theory deductively (Fassin et al., 2015). Quantitative research is not beneficial for researchers when ideas on the subject are still in development (Hinz, 2012). Additionally, the quantitative method is not ideal when the subject is not well known, or when specific variables are not available to test (Reynolds, 2014). The lack of knowledge of why international business managers establish a business case before implementing sustainability necessitates a qualitative study to ask probing questions.

The complex reasons to develop a business case for sustainability before incorporating sustainability makes the single case study design an appropriate choice. The single case study design vividly allows this researcher to understand why managers develop a business case before incorporating sustainability in the context of the process (Hinz, 2012). Phenomenologies help to discover the essence of an experience (Merriam, 2009). The phenomenological design is ineffective in this study because the aim of this study includes exploring the breadth of experiences that take place and not the essence of those experiences. The objective of researchers when using grounded theory is to build a theorem or address processes that change over time (Merriam, 2009). Building a theory is inappropriate in the context of this study because discussions about the practical applications of sustainability at firms designed sustainably from inception are not yet pervasive. Why managers develop a business case before implementing sustainability does not have clear boundaries between the phenomenon and the context, so a single case study makes the most sense (Hinz, 2014).

Research Question

The focus of this study is to expand existing research on the business case for sustainability. The intent is to learn why international business managers set up a business case for sustainability before they incorporate sustainability. The overarching question is: What factors contribute to the decision process to establish a business case

for sustainability before implementing sustainable elements?

Interview Questions

There will be 20 individual interviews. These are the seven interview questions:

1. Why do not international business managers establish a business case for
    sustainability before they incorporate sustainability?

2. Why do international business managers develop a business case for
    sustainability before they incorporate sustainability?

3. How do not internal factors contribute to the decision process to develop a
    business case for sustainability before implementing sustainable elements?

4. How do internal factors contribute to the decision process to establish a
    business case for sustainability before implementing sustainable features?

5. How do not external factors contribute to the decision process to set up a
    business case for sustainability before implementing sustainable features?

6. How do external factors contribute to the decision process to establish a
    business case for sustainability before implementing sustainable elements?

7. Why or how would anything else influence processes international
    business managers use to develop a business case for sustainability before
    implementing sustainable features?

Conceptual Framework

Internal and external interdependencies between organizational systems and

environmental systems establish the conceptual framework for the business case for sustainability (Ping, 2014). Those interdependencies are best explored using the conceptual framework of general system theory (systems theory) defined by Ludwig von Bertalanffy in 1947. Systems theory is a logical mathematical field with general principles that apply to systems in general (von Bertalanffy, 1972). Interconnected elements comprise systems so systems behave as designed (Shen, 2014). Although systems are isolatable, systems rely upon inputs for outputs (Andrade, 2015). Regardless of size, problems of smaller systems are often experienced in larger systems because commonality is a feature of systems (Perez-Vega, Ortega-Rivas, Salmeron-Ochoa, & Sharratt, 2013).

Systems theory as a lens helps this researcher see interconnections between individual parts (Shen, 2014). This researcher can see how the microsystem of the organization is connected to the macro environmental system using systems theory. The exercise of understanding the interconnectedness of the internal and external systems enables this researcher to gain a better understanding of the components and their relationships. The organizational and environmental sustainability systems parts and their connections may influence decision processes at a company with a business case for sustainability. Systems theory, as the conceptual framework for this study, is the lens that enables this researcher to identify why international business managers develop a business case for sustainability before incorporating sustainability.

Operational Definitions

The overarching concepts in this study are business case, and sustainability. Below are definitions of terms related to those concepts.

Business case. Perceived practical benefits (Swaim, Maloni, Napshin, & Henley, 2014).

Certified organic. Certification process where a producer or handler is approved by an accredited certifying agent as being in compliance with the United States Department of Agriculture (USDA) National Organic Program (NOP) regulations and is then authorized to sell, label, or represent products as being certified organic (Certified organic, 2010).

Corporate social responsibility (CSR). Compliance- and profit-driven internal focus on self-enhancement, caring with an active role in the community and charitable donations, and synergistic and holistic community engagement where goals and strategies are entwined (Wood, 2014).

Economic justice. Existence of opportunities for meaningful work and employment and the dispensation of fair rewards for the productive activities of individuals (Baudot, 2006).

Environmental justice. (a) Fair treatment and meaningful involvement of all people regardless of race, color, national origin, or income with respect to the development, implementation, and enforcement of environmental laws, regulations and policies; (b) achieved when everyone enjoys the same degree of protection from environmental and health hazards and equal access to the decision-making process to have a healthy environment to live, learn, and work in (Environmental justice, 2014).

Leadership in energy and environmental design (LEED). Developed by the United States Green Building Council (USGBC), LEED is an internationally recognized green building certification system providing third-party verification that a building or community is designed and built using strategies aimed at saving money and resources, and have a positive impact on the health of occupants while promoting renewable, clean energy (LEED, 2014).

Organic. Labeling term that indicates agricultural product has been produced through approved methods that integrate cultural, biological, and mechanical processes that foster cycling of resources to promote ecological balance and conserve biodiversity (Organic, 2014).

Social justice. Each person should have equal rights to the most extensive liberties consistent with other people enjoying the same liberties; inequalities should be arranged so that they will be to everyone's advantage so that no one is blocked from occupying any position (Bankston, 2010).

Sustainability. Conservation, deployment, and reuse of resources in responsible ways (Malhotra, Melville, & Watson, 2013)

Assumptions, Limitations, and Delimitations

This subsection is about the assumptions, limitations and delimitations regarding the why international business managers develop a business case for sustainability before incorporating sustainability. Assumptions are unverified inferences, limitations are weaknesses in the design of the study, and delimitations are the bounds of the study (Dean, 2014).

Assumptions

Interviewees of the consultancy group require their clients to have a business case for sustainability before the consultants assist the entrepreneurs. One assumption critical to the validity of this study is the experts understand why they set up a business case for sustainability before they incorporate sustainability themselves (Abu, Ritchie, & Jones, 2012). Given that the consultants help other entrepreneurs through the entire business process, it is also assumed the experts seek to understand why the aspiring entrepreneurs established a business case before starting their sustainably designed businesses (Zhang & Zhang, 2014).

It is possible the international business consultants developed a business case for sustainability before implementing sustainability without knowing why they decided to do so. It is also possible the experts do not seek to understand why their clients chose to establish a business case prior to setting up a company with a sustainable business model. Since these scenarios are possible, consultants will have time to reflect on the interview questions before the interview. This researcher will send the interview questions a week in advance of our meeting, and confirm our meeting time and date. Even if the consultants know why they and their clients established a business case for sustainability before implementing sustainability, some people have difficulty articulating their answers spontaneously. In any event, delivery of the interview questions in advance of the meeting will mitigate those challenges.

Limitations

There are three limitations to this study. The design is the 1st limitation (Rueede & Kreutzer, 2015). Since this study is a single case study, the research is based on information obtained from one company. A case study including leaders of several companies may provide different results. The 2nd limitation is the quantity and quality of interviewees. There will be 20 participants in this study, and all of them are experts. Assistants and other subordinates to the consultants, regardless that they may have valuable insight, will not be interviewed (Reynolds, 2014). The 3rd limitation for this study is the number of researchers. This researcher is the only investigator. Because there is only one researcher, this study lacks the diversity of knowledge, skills, abilities, and experiences that multiple team members would bring to a project (Reale, 2014). Consequently, the full depth and breadth potential of this study may not be reached.

Delimitations

Delimitations are the bounds and scope a researcher sets in a study. Bounds are like a fence. Investigators focus on what is inside of the fence (Merriam, 2009). The scope is like a researcher looking through a microscope at the fenced-in area of the study. The researcher studies what the researcher sees through the lens, even though there is much more outside the view of the scope.

The bounds of this study are one consulting firm comprised of 59 internationally experienced brand development experts (Jesper, Kristin, & Arlbjørn, 2013). The subject company is a consulting firm located on the East Coast of the United States of America.

Members of the consulting firm have established a business case for sustainability before incorporating sustainability.

The scope of this study is 20 of the brand development professionals. Included will be the approved responses from each of the 20 individually interviewed experts. This researcher is not observing the professionals performing their job functions, so derived data collection is from interviews (Reynolds, 2014).

Significance of the Study

This study is about why international business managers develop a business case for sustainability before they incorporate sustainability. This study is valuable to business leaders because there may not be any literature about practitioners that had the foresight to develop a business case before incorporating sustainability. This study builds on the work of previous researchers that investigated the work of business leaders who transitioned their companies to include sustainable practices.

Contribution to Business Practice

One-fifth of business leaders that deploy sustainability tactics without a business case for sustainability decrease their profits (Eccles & Serafeim, 2013). Developing a framework for action from the philosophical ideas of sustainability is challenging when few people have been through a similar process (Amodeo, 2005). More studies are needed to improve the efficacy of a practice and create another reference point for senior executives and other managers that desire to make their organizations sustainable (Holliday, 2010). This doctoral study is a single case study designed to add to the body of literature by describing why international business managers establish a business case for sustainability before incorporating sustainability. This study is a positive contribution to the body of literature regarding sustainability because this is the first study about business leaders that developed businesses cases for sustainability before starting sustainability initiatives. The gap to reduce in the literature is the difference between justifications of managers for business cases at firms transitioning to sustainability and justifications of managers for business cases at firms where sustainability was part of their original business plan. Business leaders that have a business case for sustainability may be better positioned to profit from their sustainability initiatives.

Implications for Social Change

Sustainability is often not visible, but the effects of unsustainability are distinct. Effects of unsustainability include strikes, absenteeism, resignations, obstructive behaviors (Mbah & Ifeanyi, 2012), environmental degradation (Brown, 2012), and public protest (Shuv-Ami, 2013). However, problems such as those often seem to be the problems of other people, negating the need to establish a business case before incorporating sustainability (Hahn, Pinkse, Preuss, & Figge, 2015). Without a clear understanding of why to develop a business case, development of a business case for sustainability is not a priority. Neglecting aspects of sustainability such as social justice, economic justice, and environmental justice, may cause manageable threats to exacerbate into socially, economically, and environmentally expensive problems. Organizational leaders conscious of the negative externalities associated with unsustainable human resource management may be better positioned to minimize harmful effects on their employees, family members, and communities (Mariappanadar, 2012). Managers that are adept at sustainability engage organizational stakeholders, and foster an innovative spirit to create or maintain a competitive advantage (Reynolds, 2014). In short, developing a business case for sustainability before incorporating sustainable elements can create a mutually beneficial working environment by learning from others and acting accordingly. Following this subsection is comprehensive synthesis and review of the literature.

A Review of the Professional and Academic Literature

The purpose of this qualitative single case study is to learn why international business managers establish a business case for sustainability before they incorporate sustainability. This researcher exhaustively reviewed the literature to gain a better understanding of why international business managers define their business case for sustainability before implementing some sustainable element. Research databases used in this study are EBSCOhost and ProQuest. Search terms were *system theory*, *organizational sustainability*, and *environmental sustainability*. All 60 references in this literature review are from scholarly peer-reviewed journals. Of those citations, 59 are published 2012 or after, so 98% of the references in this literature review are published within five years of publication of this study. Through thorough reviews of the literature, this researcher was able to develop three major themes: (1) systems thinking, (2) internal interdependencies, and (3) external interdependencies.

This literature review begins with an exploration of the conceptual framework, systems thinking. Managers, with a thorough understanding of the systems thinking conceptual framework, are better positioned to conceptualize connections, causes, and effects. The ability to see the interplay between a part of a system and a larger system is a skill that enables managers to see how their micro-organizational system connects with the macro-environmental system. The research by Von Bertalanffy (1972) provides the conceptual framework for this study of why international managers develop a business case for sustainability before incorporating sustainability. The systems thinking subsection starts with an overview of what systems theory is. Then, described in several paragraphs, are use and application of systems thinking. Use and application paragraphs include discussions of theory, problem solving, leadership, decision making, and analysis. The systems thinking discussion ends with a shifts paragraph that includes descriptions of managerial barriers to proper utilization of systems thinking.

Overview. Systems are everywhere, and range from particulate to galactic (Ping, 2014). Systems are observable wholes, comprised of elements, and interact with the environment (Sehu & Dobric, 2014). Wholes cannot be whole without the sum of their parts (von Bertalanffy, 1972). In systems, parts of the whole influence behaviors in other aspects, and behaviors of each aspect influence behavior of the whole (Shen, 2014). Systems have mutual connections and restrictions, with specific functions that comprise the organic whole (Ping, 2014). Even though the parts may act in contradiction to one another, the parts are still members of a larger system (von Bertalanffy, 1972). Kotecha, Diwekar, and Cabezas (2013) subsume many of the relationships between various components of the ecosystem can be nonlinear, intertwined, and non-intuitive. Andrade (2015) identified interactions as non-linear, incompressible, and cannot be represented by smaller similar systems. The interdisciplinary nature of systems theory allows individual systems to coexist in the collective whole (von Bertalanffy, 1972). The collection of elements in a system connects with- and restricts-each other (Ping, 2014). Planet Earth is a dynamic system, and humans rely on natural Earth processes for their well-being (Storsletten & Jakobsen, 2015). Ping (2014) advocated that system analysis provides a scientific theory and method for humans to understand objectively the changing world from the viewpoint of the system. Real systems are discrete, and definable by their cohesion (von Bertalanffy, 1972). It is the collection and relations of elements that determine the concrete structure of a system with a particular function (Ping, 2014). Systems are interdependent, dynamic, and composed of many factors with complicated relationships that interact with each other (Ping, 2014). Perez-Vega et al. (2013) noted part of the philosophical basis for system theory is the study of common properties in different objects. Immediately following this overview paragraph are common properties, and other theory aspects of system theory.

Theory. Shen (2014) identified four commonalities across systems thinking: (1) making distinctions (2) recognizing interrelationships (3) organizing part-whole systems and (4) taking multiple perspectives. Interdependence is an internal behavior while interaction with the environment is an external function (von Bertalanffy, 1972). Sehu and Dobric (2014) observed higher education institutions and employers as systems cooperatively working for economic development by providing educated workers and places for graduates to work. Institutions and firms serve as meeting places for constituents and become social systems with intercommunications to generate new properties and attributes (Chassagnon, 2014). Within the meeting places, department representatives interact with each other, naturally self-alternating to adapt to changes

(Sehu & Dobric, 2014). A company, like a complex collective, autopoietically exists

through the interactions of its constituents (Chassagnon, 2014). Ardichvili (2012)

asserted that human resource development is part of a larger system comprised of the

cognate disciplines of sustainability, corporate social responsibility, and business ethics.

Von Bertalanaffy (1972) described dynamical system theory as internal and external

changes in systems over time. Ardichvili (2012) saw systems theory as a foundational

concept for human resource development to understand the systemic nature of the

interrelations of the economy, the environment, and society. Ardichvili (2012)

prognosticated unbalanced subsystems, because of overuse, could cause instability in

some other system or eventual collapse of the subsystem. Sustainable businesses need

sustainable human and environmental resources (Ardichvili, 2012). Hahn, Pinkse,

Preuss, and Figge (2015) posited organizational leaders alone may not be able to achieve

sustainability in their organizations. Rather, sustainability in organizations is supported

by design and structure (Ardichvili, 2012). Ping (2014) asserted building a systematic

social responsibility system more adequately fulfills social responsibility objectives,

better reflects social responsibility values, and aids in the fruition of the sustainable

development of enterprises. Ping (2014) also outlined the corporate social responsibility

theory system. Social systems have internal conditions, external conditions, energy and

information exchanges, current interests, and long-term interests (Ping, 2014). More is

not always better; and, Human Resource Development (HRD) should foster societies,

organizations, and individuals that achieve success and satisfaction from more than solely financial metrics (Ardichvili, 2012). However, sustainability in society should not come at the expense of organizations or individuals and vice versa, because that is inherently unsustainable (Ardichvili, 2012). Likewise, one part of a system cannot indefinitely grow while other segments of the system do not grow (Ardichvili, 2012). The design and structure of a stable system will not be affected by perturbations (von Bertalanffy, 1972). Ping (2014) expounded on that thought, postulating the order of a system controls relationships, and enables stable contact between each factor. When system balance is upset, practitioners solve problems by studying the multitude of variables and their interrelationships in systems (von Bertalanffy, 1972).

Problem-solving. System thinking can be useful for decision makers in quandary solving to determine the nature of a problem, the cause, explore feasible solutions, and compare solutions to a standard (Ping, 2014). Sehu and Dobric (2014) furthered that concept; when there is a problem in an organization, it is possible the cause of the problem is a lack of a systematic approach. Using system analysis, researchers can observe the complexity of predicaments, and develop a methodology to study the vicissitude (Perez-Vega et al., 2013). Scientifically, through the use of mathematics, computers, and applications, researchers can use system analysis to plan, organize, and manage study strategy for complex problems (Ping, 2014). Issues that arise while trying to solve problems are due to multiple alternative sets and choices criteria that create uncertainty regarding solutions to complex situations (Perez-Vega et al., 2013). One of the main reasons for imbroglio is the lack of awareness of the interconnectedness, interdependencies, and interactions of complex factors and processes that form whole complex systems (Perez-Vega et al., 2013). Part of the challenge of system thinking is trying to recognize how coordinated systems exist on purpose, terms, and expected results (Perez-Vega et al., 2013). However, because of the interconnected nature of systems and subsystems, systems are inherently open, so definitions act merely as a framing apparatus (Andrade, 2015). Critical thinking can be used to assess or evaluate systems to identify substantive flaws or missing links; creative thinking can be useful to come-up with original ideas that resolve flaws or add value, and design thinking can be appropriate for coordination and implementation (Adu-Febiri, 2014). When there is a paucity of data or random uncertainty, Grey system theory can be effective to produce satisfactory outcomes (Bai & Sarkis, 2013). Another useful application of Grey system theory is analysis and modeling in supply chain management, economics, agriculture, medicine, geography, and disasters (Bai & Sarkis, 2013). The multiplicity of approaches to systems theory enables practitioners to see connections that were otherwise overlooked (von Bertalanffy, 1972). However, results of a scenario analysis should be considered with caution because forecasts, projections, and predictions may not transpire as originally planned (Kotecha, Diwekar, & Cabezas, 2013). Unique challenges, such as these mentioned in this paragraph, create new demands, and require distinctive forms of leadership (Wolfgramm et al., 2015).

Leadership. Some organizational leaders embrace the systems approach; while others either reject, or are unaware, of the applicability of systems theory to the business environment. The deliberate or unwitting disdain for systems thinking does not make systems theory irrelevant (von Bertalanffy, 1972). Like gravity, if one respects it, rejects it, or is unaware of it, systems theory will eventually be made known in consequence of life doings. The sagacious organizational leader recognizes the relevance of the systems approach, and applies it aproposly. Thereby, the prudent leader responsibly utilizes limited available resources, and is primed for aftereffects (von Bertalanffy, 1972). Activities that require more than one person require organization (Chassagnon, 2014). Organizational leaders should be prepared to work with and manage diverse character types to help them achieve their full potential, and stakeholders may have competing or conflicting interests that need to be balanced (Storsletten & Jakobsen, 2015). Leadership that lacks purposiveness, motivation, will, intentionality, or initiative, may be inhibited to direct change (Wolfgramm et al., 2015). Where leaders or leadership teams have deficits, they may pursue agency relationships to act on their behalf (Wolfgramm, Flynn-Colemann, & Conroy, 2015). Wolfgramm, Flynn-Colemann, and Conroy (2015) proposed ethical leaders have characteristics that include people orientation, concern for sustainability, society, and the environment, and can address those concerns through fairness, power sharing, and integrity. For societal and organizational success in achieving sustainability, there must be buy-in from individuals at-large (Ardichvili, 2012). As actors in the larger system, organizational leaders' success in sustainability is limited by the sustainability achieved in the larger system (Hahn et al., 2015). Leaders that have sustainability-focused mindsets and competencies can influence individuals by promoting sustainability through their organizational culture (Ardichvili, 2012). Foci on responsibility, and sustainability, indicate leadership has a long-term view of success (Wolfgramm et al., 2015). Ardichvili (2012) opined sustainability proliferation may require post-conventional moral development, where balancing rights and respect for all is universal, and guides decision-making (Ardichvili, 2012). Reflection, creativity, and continuous learning through action learning, field projects, and knowledge management, can also influence sustainability adoption (Ardichvili, 2012). Although, clearly seeing a system or aspects of a system can be convoluted by disembodied leadership, making it difficult to do the right thing (Wolfgramm et al., 2015). Reflection on actions can be useful to discern meaning and build integrity (Robinson, 2015). Astutely, an organizational leader utilizes systems thinking as a vetting tool in the decision process afore an undertaking.

Decision making. Before leaders make any decision, it is necessary to develop procedures to explain and evaluate the essence of what is to be solved (Perez-Vega et al., 2013). For decision-making regarding social systems, an optimal solution satisfies current and future interests (Ping, 2014). Business mindsets tend to be either to do what is best for business, or best for the environment; obversely, business leaders can strive to do what is best for business and best for the environment (Glavas & Mish, 2015). Carson et al. (2015) asserted leaders should also pay attention to internal signals and make changes accordingly. However, local benefits in a subsystem may be inconsistent or contrary to the overall efficiency of the system (Ping, 2014). For full efficiency and optimization, local benefits should be sacrificed for the advancement of the larger system (Ping, 2014). System analysis methodologies give structure to decision-making strategies to aid exploration of interrelations and connectivity among varying elements, restrictions, and requirements (Perez-Vega et al., 2013).

Analysis. System analysis is a study of coordinating efforts in the microsystem for optimal design and operation of the macrosystem (Ping, 2014). System analysis, as a scientific methodology, is a way to study structure, logical organization, properties, and characteristics of complex systems (Perez-Vega et al., 2013). The essence of the system method is to use logical thought, mathematical models, and computers for system analysis and system design to realize the model, and optimize the system (Ping, 2014). Kotecha, Diwekar, and Cabezas (2013) appreciated the modeling feature of systems theory to discern the dynamics of a system without disturbing the actual system. System analysis has diverse applicability for optimization, and may become an indispensable tool for managers in decision-making processes in science, technology, liberal arts, and economics (Ping, 2014). Because of the complex nature of systems, system analysis will have the best results when researchers use both quantitative and qualitative methods (Ping, 2014). Human welfare depends on the application of system analyses for the rational use of global material, power, and information resources (Perez-Vega et al., 2013).

Shifts. Research by Ardichvili (2012) shows a global shift from economic and organizational growth, toward balanced and sustainable practices and philosophy in business strategy, and HRD is needed. Antecedents for the shift include changing economic realities, and corresponding organizational practices (Ardichvili, 2012). Zeng (2014) and Wolfgramm et al. (2015) wrote about challenges in enterprises transitioning through institutional changes because of heavy reliance on already clearly established older systems. Low desire, and resistance to institutional change, require a strong top-down commitment to lead desired systemic changes (Zeng, 2014). However, developing a systems approach or a sustainability objective can be encumbered by inflexible bureaucracies, hyperpoliticized environments, intellectual silos, rigid hierarchical structures, and asymmetrical power relations (Wolfgramm et al., 2015). Differing political ideologies, associated policies, oversight, and tax structures, also create constraints that limit autonomy (Zeng, 2014). Additionally, there may be disinterest, disillusionment, cynicism, skepticism, or other dogmatic resistance to change (Wolfgramm et al., 2015). Egoism, elitism, arrogance, technocracy, competitive altruism, institutional narcissism, fanaticism without reason, or leaders with other pressing priorities could also produce barriers and complexities to enactment (Wolfgramm et al., 2015). Risk mitigation or traditional growth strategies may also be hindrances (Wolfgramm et al., 2015). Sometimes, there are simply funding deficits or other competitive pressures to trump sustainability initiatives (Wolfgramm et al., 2015). Zeng (2014) identified market uncertainties make effective management of those uncertainties dampering. Furthermore, global institutions may have a debilitating effect on institutional development (Zeng, 2014). Despite all of the aforementioned blockades and impediments, lone sustainability champions may still attempt to persevere in the face of adversity (Wolfgramm et al., 2015). The varying demands amongst all of the stakeholders can be threatening or intimidating, but taking the time to identify and understand the tensions, can enable practical management of the tensions (Hahn et al., 2015).

That concludes the systems thinking subsection. The systems subsection began with a general discussion of systems theory. Then this researcher unraveled use and application of systems theory through the discourse of problem-solving, leadership, decision making, analysis, shifts and managerial barriers to proper utilization of systems thinking. Next, is an examination of internal interdependencies as an aspect of systems thinking. Internal interdependencies may affect adoption of a business case for sustainability before incorporating sustainability. This internal interdependencies discussion starts with a continued explication of systems, segues through competition and financial considerations, and closes with values and reputation ponderances.

Systems. Zeidan, Boechat, and Fleury (2015) explained, there are external and internal practices related to sustainability. External practices, are communication with shareholders and other stakeholders, and mitigation of corporate externalities (Zeidan, Boechat, & Fleury, 2015). Internal practices relate to sustainability, criteria for risk management models, and how management practices change regarding sustainability issues (Zeidan et al., 2015). Attempting to accomplish economic, environmental, and social targets simultaneously creates mutually dependent objectives, which could create a high risk of unintended consequences because a solution to one issue could create a problem elsewhere (Hahn et al., 2015). Seeking a balance between the opposing strategies of efficiency and resilience is conflicting, but discussions between the different actors can bring about creative solutions that may engender benefits greater than the individual strategies alone (Hahn et al., 2015). Organizational leaders that develop dynamic capabilities can integrate, build, and reconfigure internal and external competencies to address rapidly changing environments (Glavas & Mish, 2015).

Organizational leaders of people-planet-profit, also known as triple bottom line (TBL)

TBL firms, integrate the external social and environmental contexts as central missions

for the companies they handle (Glavas & Mish, 2015). Additionally, TBL leaders do not

draw a clear boundary between their firms and the environment (Glavas & Mish, 2015).

At TBL firms, social, environmental, and economic performance is equally measured and

rewarded, so the institutional context is an indispensable foundation of everyday business

(Glavas & Mish, 2015). Guerci et al. (2015) opined organizational climate, i.e. the

collection of attitudes, feelings, and behaviors, reflect shared perceptions employees have

regarding policies, practices, and procedures that management rewards, supports, and

expects. Organizational climates reflect, and influence, what constitutes appropriate

employee decision-making (Guerci et al., 2015). Architecture too can be used to create

visual cues that symbolize shared values (Frerichs et al., 2015). Frerichs et al., (2015)

stated programming and practices are central components necessary to drive change.

When overcoming barriers such as competing priorities and insufficient financial

resources, programming and practices can be powerful reinforcing feedback loops to

provoke organizational change that can influence organizational sustainability (Frerichs

et al., 2015). Programs, not implemented with care, may have unintentional undesired

effects on employees, and superficial ethics programs may do more harm than good

(Maclean et al., 2015). Decoupling a central program will have greater ill effects than

decoupling ancillary programs (Maclean et al., 2015). Organizational leaders should be

aware that behavior is a manifestation of personality (Storsletten & Jakobsen, 2015).

However, like most aspects of social science, there may be no definitives, and norms are subject to change (Storsletten & Jakobsen, 2015). Robinson (2015) researched why people would be interested in acting responsibly, and discussed consequentialism. People may responsibly choose to act because they have a consequentialist mentality; meaning, they choose to undertake with purpose because they are interested in a desirable result. Robinson (2015) described some consequentialist desires are the betterment of the environment or improving the quality of life (Robinson, 2015). Robinson (2015) construed that some people may feel obligated personally, or that responsibly acting is a duty, as a shared social response. Having an open dialog enables learning, and can improve transparency, and accountability (Robinson, 2015). Open dialog with competitors can be an opportunity to share best practices in challenging economic environments.

Competition. In high-cost regions, organizational leaders can improve their competitive ability by projecting high economic-social value, or they can lower costs by increasing efficiencies (Carson, Hagen, & Sethi, 2015). Political, financial, labor, education, and cultural systems transformations from local to global have led to explicit CSR (Carson et al., 2015). Markets can become increasingly similar in international business because business leaders incorporate the same popular formal elements (Carson et al., 2015). Organizational leaders can manage their legitimacy reactively by adapting to external expectations, or actively by strategically gaining public support (Panwar et al., 2014). Internal changes can also be inspired by a customer request, challenge, pressure, or other inquiry (Carson et al., 2015). Hahn et al. (2015) asserted corporate sustainability requires organizational leaders to address interconnected and interdependent economic, environmental, and social concerns at different levels. Leaders with a TBL orientation strive for organization-wide generation of market intelligence regarding current and future social, environmental, and economic system needs, and dissemination of that information for organization-wide responsiveness (Glavas & Mish, 2015). Information gathering and responsiveness can be the instruments of the vanguard for improved financials.

Financial. Economics is usually prioritized over environmental and social concerns; although, there can be financial benefits when environmental or social concerns become the priority (Hahn et al., 2015). CSR may affect the cost of capital, and some lenders may react positively to CSR practices (Zeidan et al., 2015). Environmental related advantageous behaviors are leveraging waste management, incorporating environmental awareness into product design, pursuing environmental management systems, and developing environmentally friendly supply chains (Asiri, 2015). In instrumental logic, the natural environment and social considerations are vetted through a profit maximization lens (Hahn et al., 2015). Zeidan et al. (2015) identified five reasons leaders incorporate sustainability: (1) event-related integration (2) new banking strategy (3) value driver (4) public mission and (5) client requirement. Storsletten and Jakobsen (2015) mentioned responsible organizational leaders seek a profit to ensure enough liquidity to secure future investments. Leaders with a resource-based view (RBV) work toward a competitive advantage by seeking control of valuable, rare, inimitable, and non-substitutable resources (VRIO framework) (Glavas & Mish, 2015). Hahn et al. (2015)

observed there can be organizational tension when environmental and social aspects do not make financial sense. Prust et al. (2015) found there are several coping tactics organizational leaders can use during times where budget restrictions or cuts are necessary. Organizational leaders have coped with budget cuts by identifying additional sources of revenue and decreasing use of services paid-for and services provided pro bono (Prust et al., 2015). Staffing related cost-cutting measures include eliminating personnel, adjusting hours worked, changing responsibilities and adjusting salaries (Prust et al., 2015). Although some staffing related cost-cutting measures may be tempting to make permanent, there could be long-term impacts on staff morale, retention, and quality of services (Prust et al., 2015). Shareholder value maximization as the primary aim of organizational leaders used to be considered the only purpose that could withstand the competitive pressures of the marketplace; however, the success of TBL firms shows alternative models can also be viable options (Glavas & Mish, 2015). Heretofore, beneficial exchanges transpire and continue to transpire when organizational leaders can adequately understand customer perception of value, and deliver products that functionally and emotionally satisfy their customers (Bahar, Alam, Mahfuz, & Khar, 2015). Using signaling theory, wealth, profitability, or health events announced 25 to 50 days in advance of the event may have significant positive effects on company performance (Asiri, 2015). Asiri (2015) delineated, events can include demergers, larger spin-offs, tax friendly divestments, ethical behaviors, adopting new technologies, spinoffs that lead to improved industrial focus, and expansion of investments in new projects.

Other aspects of organizational interdependence that affect financial deliberations are individual and collective values.

Values. Guerci, Radaelli, Siletti, Cirella, and Rami Shani (2015) postulated dysfunctional ethical environments are one of the main reasons for illegal or unethical behaviors. Local organizational ethical climates can be egoistic for the benefit of the individual, benevolent with perceived benefits for others, and principled as formally or informally established within the organization (Guerci et al., 2015). Carson, Hagen, & Sethi (2015) continued that asseveration contending; managerial perspectives can range from good-for-me, to good-for-us, to good-for-everyone. When organizational leaders publish a Code of Business Conduct and Ethics or other similar documents, but do not follow published guidelines, stakeholders may feel suspicion, disillusionment, disgust, cynicism, and may resign (Maclean, Litzky, & Holderness, 2015). Maclean, Litzky, and Holderness (2015) interpreted this phenomenon, known as decoupling, as a disconnection between symbolic adoption to appease external stakeholders and substantive implementation, thereby affirming a *business as usual* environment. Bahar, Alam, Mahfuz, and Khar (2015) construed values are the benefits received for the costs paid. Bahar et al. (2015) asserted benefits are functional, emotional, and determined by the customer, not the company. However, internal interdependencies and needs should appropriately be balanced with external needs of the local community to generate a win-win scenario (Carson et al., 2015). Establishing a long-term explicitly-stated sustainability mission insulates the independence of the organization from stakeholders that may try to manipulate the organizational direction (Hahn et al., 2015). Increased expressiveness of values allows organizational leaders to position their companies to gain, maintain, or repair their legitimacy (Carson et al., 2015). The proactive approach incorporates voluntary practices that go beyond mere regulatory compliance (Hahn et al., 2015). Glavas and Mish (2015) found organizational leaders that have TBL foci strive to secure imitable, commonly found, substitutable sustainable resources and work toward collaborative rather than competitive relationships. Hahn et al. (2015) insisted top management tasked with long-term sustainability concerns enable lower level managers to be more forward looking. Glavas and Mish (2015) presumed organizational leaders that have TBL foci create win-win synergies between economic, social, and environmental goals and can secure sustainability economically, socially, and environmentally simultaneously. Organizational leaders that openly share what they know, sustainably have smaller degrees of asymmetry than organizational leaders that know more than they are willing to share with their stakeholders (Lu & Chueh, 2015). Proactive leaders with TBL foci consider the environment and actively work to shape it by forming new markets, influencing peers, and changing social perceptions (Glavas & Mish, 2015).

Reputation. CSR is one way organizational leaders build reputational capital and legitimacy for their organization (Panwar, Paul, Nybakk, Hansen & Thompson, 2014). Legitimization is the deliberate effort to ensure relevance regarding some issue and eschew association with some other matter (Rueede & Kreutzer, 2015). CSR has become a strategic tool to enhance corporate reputation and public trust for the corporation (Carson et al., 2015). Rueede and Kreutzer (2015) opined legitimization efforts without an audience lose value and meaning, given that legitimacy is a product of the social judgment by stakeholders. Past CSR performance, the effectiveness of CSR communication strategy, and public perception of the subject company's industry sector, all influence legitimacy of CSR claims (Panwar et al., 2014). After purpose is defined and accepted internally, then legitimization efforts can extend outside of the organization to earn an endorsement from the broader context (Rueede & Kreutzer, 2015). Panwar et al. (2014) prognosticated CSR claims do not insure organizations against corporate scandals and ethical shortcomings. However, proactive management can lead to critical acclaim that overshadows internal oversights (Carson et al., 2015). Panwar, Paul, Nybakk, Hansen, and Thompson (2014) identified positive perceptions of legitimacy can contribute to investor appeal. Rueede and Kreutzer (2015) perorated aspects or areas of the organization that needs legitimization may change; correspondingly, approval audiences may also change. An effective means to earn legitimacy gains in CSR is to develop a strategic alliance with organizational leaders that already have a specialization in that area (Rueede & Kreutzer, 2015). Other benefits of accreditation through CSR include consumer trust and patronage, and existing and future employee appeal (Panwar et al., 2014). Along with organizational legitimacy, reputation management regarding environmental management may influence an organizational leader's ability to attract and retain employees with the right skill sets (Storsletten & Jakobsen, 2015).

This researcher just concluded internal interdependencies discussion subsection. In that part, this researcher further described the integral role of systems. Other themes this researcher covered in internal interdependencies are competition from an organizational view, financial considerations, and critical discussions of the roles of values and reputation. Following this subsection, this researcher will investigate external interdependencies as it relates to organizational leaders desire to establish a business case for sustainability before incorporating sustainability. Continuing as before, this researcher begins the external interdependencies subsection by describing the integral role of systems thinking. Systematic interdependencies in business administration become more apparent in this area as this researcher's critical analysis reveals content that can be categorized under the same themes: competition, financial, values, and reputation. This researcher concludes external interdependencies with insights regarding leadership and government.

System. Members of society allow organizations to operate as long as there are perceived benefits to society (Panwar et al., 2014). Organizational veracity can be pragmatic to benefit stakeholders, cognitive with a shared social understanding of the necessity of the organization, and normative/moral for a social purpose (Panwar et al., 2014). Organizational leaders that feel they are part of a greater whole may make decisions that all-encompassingly benefit the firm, society, and the environment (Glavas & Mish, 2015). Social responsibility orientation includes individualistic and egalitarian values; where economic inequalities are balanced by meeting basic needs of people, including redressing unfair social inequalities (Panwar et al., 2014). Some organizational leaders believe the only way to achieve sustainability for the planet and society is to work together (Glavas & Mish, 2015). Business leaders that have organizational and environmental interests may prefer to work with other business leaders that have organizational and environmental interests as priorities (Glavas & Mish, 2015). Poor

corporate citizens are not democratic in their decision-making structures, do not

transparently disclose organizational activities, do not align their interests with societal

interests, and are not accountable for most of the negative externalities they generate

(Morsing & Roepstorff, 2015). Fassin et al. (2015) found some managers have a sincere

conviction for CSR while others merely use CSR for a public relations benefit. In

countries where notions of individual responsibility are strong, organizational leaders are

apt to implement corporate social action (CSA) plans and not just signal implementation,

so they are less likely to greenwash (Roulet & Touboul, 2015). Jacobson et al.(2015)

asserted systematic examination of business processes can reduce waste, and costs

associated with those wastes. An important sustainability consideration is to envisage

current inputs and outputs, and question what would happen if a portion was removed or

replaced (Lampikoski et al., 2014). Glavas and Mish (2015) contended building a new

TBL market requires system-wide collaboration including the full supply chain, and

support from local, federal, and non-governmental organizations. Maletic et al. (2014)

predicated one of the most important parts of sustainability innovation is to include

stakeholders in development discussions to ensure needs fulfillment. Public recognition

of apparent failures creates an opportunity for leaders to network internally and

externally, to identify cooperatively, and implement solutions (Glavas & Mish, 2015).

Unexpected disturbances addressed individually, or systematic assessment of the

situation, should include contextual, communal, historical contexts, and processes

(Wexler et al., 2015). Current practices may be improved by learning from stakeholders through participatory action research (Wexler et al., 2015). After efficiencies of processes become optimized, then organizational leaders can begin exploring supplemental revenue streams (Jacobson et al., 2015). Maletic, Maletic, Dahlgaard, Dahlgaard-Park, and Gomiscek (2014) ascertained developing competencies for sustainability innovation can foster a competitive advantage. A sustainability innovation program may be able to help organizational leaders respond to needs and expectations of varying stakeholders (Maletic, Maletic, Dahlgaard, Dahlgaard-Park, & Gomiscek, 2014). Stakeholders tend to make meaning of their workplace with shared understandings of central, distinctive, and enduring elements; likewise, those elements reinforce their identity negotiations (Morsing & Roepstorff, 2015). An aspect of public administration is difficulty identifying root causes because of interdependencies (Gore, 2014). Fassin et al. (2015) portend CSR is onerous to study alone because of practices that overlap such as ethics, sustainability, stakeholder management, and corporate governance. Social- and religious-traditions can also influence conceptualization of business ethics and CSR (Fassin et al., 2015). Multistakeholder Initiatives (MSIs), with corporate and non-corporate stakeholders, are sometimes formed to provide solutions to social and environmental problems and fill governance gaps (Moog, Spicer, & Böhm, 2015). Moog, Spicer, and Böhm (2015) realized MSIs can be an effective organizational learning tool that encourages communication and deliberation. However, membership in an MSI may cost more than the benefits received, and efforts without national, legal, or financial support may be ineffectual (Moog et al., 2015). Wexler et al. (2015) posited, passive approaches to information dissemination are usually ineffective, and managers should not rely on automatic transmission. Gore (2014) opined environmental sustainability issues occur in personal and professional contexts. Leaders that understand their environmental footprint metrics are better able to authentically and transparently communicate positive and negative aspects of their business to their stakeholders; thereby, the organizational leaders can build trust that can lead to increased customer loyalty, innovation advantages, satisfied employees, and other benefits (Glavas & Mish, 2015). Sustainability requires negotiation to balance all of the interrelated elements of the organization, and the local business environment (Nambiar & Chitty, 2014). Successful systems should also include reconciliation of conflicting interests, development of win-win solutions, and fair tradeoffs (Gore, 2014).

Competition. Family-owned businesses may have more CSR legitimacy, trust, and stakeholder loyalty than publicly traded companies (Panwar et al., 2014). A useful guide is to work on the right things instead of working on making the wrong things less bad (Malhotra, Melville, & Watson, 2013). Nambiar and Chitty (2014) averred, new approaches to sustainability can include personal agency for change, avoiding presenting sustainability as a first world concern, and discussion and execution of sustainability actionables. Allowing stakeholders to set goals actively, and providing feedback, can encourage proactive behaviors (Malhotra et al., 2013). Chuang & Gober (2015) excogitated using census data and other evidentiary metrics can create customer depth that can be used to develop prioritization. Malhotra et al. (2013) found organizational leaders that actively analyze their internal data streams can find ways to optimize social, environmental, and economic dimensions. Cai (2015) postulated pursuing growth at a more than sustainable rate can create economic burdens with more costs than benefits. Changes should include workers preferences for working times to accommodate varying needs (Brandenburg & Rebs, 2015). Malhotra et al. (2013) described transformation tools known as reflective disclosure, information democratization, output management to form a boundary for environmental impact, and delocalization. Putting current customers or prospective customers on a map provides a high-level visual orientation that can be used to assess current and future needs (Chuang & Gober, 2015). Intangible benefits of pursuing sustainable strategies are employee attraction, retention, engagement, and brand enrichment (Lampikoski et al., 2014). Peters and Romi (2015) premonished sustainability officers may improve the amount of sustainability reporting, but the quality of the reporting could be questionable without assurance. Once solutions are in action, organizational leaders should showcase and publicize products of their sustainability leaders with media coverage of public praise of sustainability champions (Nambiar & Chitty, 2014). Validating results with assurance is often dependent on use by peers and other industry pressures (Peters & Romi, 2015). Another industry pressure, a shrinking labor pool, can lead to increased production costs as a result of increased costs to attract and retain employees (Cai, 2015).

Financial. Lopatta and Kaspereit (2014) presaged sustainability pursuits can be costly activities without commensurate results. Yet, 83% of global organizational leaders consider spending on sustainability as an investment (Albrecht & Greenwald, 2014). Environmental, social, and governance issues can bring about long-term financial consequences both good and bad (Albrecht & Greenwald, 2014). Some business leaders believe by making decisions that save money now and are detrimental to the

environment, effectually deferring indirect expenses, product cost is not real unless it

includes environmental considerations (Glavas & Mish, 2015). In their study of

liberalism and coordinated markets perspectives, Roulet and Touboul (2015) found

organizational leaders tend to favor symbolic instead of substantive CSA, referred to as

greenwashing, when cultural beliefs were in favor of competition. Lopatta and Kaspereit

(2014) found investors prefer to invest in environmentally and socially riskier industries.

However, investors prefer to mitigate the risks of the firm they are investing-in through

some sustainability strategy (Lopatta & Kaspereit, 2014). The business case for

sustainability requires organizational leaders to link a sustainability initiative with a

positive financial outcome (Albrecht & Greenwald, 2014). Jacobson, Wasserman, Wu,

and Lauer (2015) identified outsourcing, reducing waste, cutting costs, optimizing

processes, and seeking additional revenue streams, requires leadership that has the vision,

will, and political courage. Organizational leaders may encourage carpooling,

ridesharing, carsharing, or a similar function when there is a push to reduce costs

(Shaheen & Bansal, 2015). Albrecht and Greenwald (2014) say organizational leaders

should focus on sustainability initiatives that have the greatest benefits to the company

and society. There is much literature that explores CSR and financial performance, but

there is not a clear business case for CSR (Fassin et al., 2015).

Values. Organizational leaders that choose business models that include social

responsibility, corporate responsibility, and sustainability, may do so because they feel

they are part of a greater whole (Glavas & Mish, 2015). Brandenburg and Rebs (2015) asserted some win-win ideas are to reduce costs in conjunction with material input, or to save energy while increasing output. Eisenbeiss, van Knippenberg, and Fahrbach (2015) presumed social learning can be an effective tool to establish and reiterate ethical standards, promote group outcomes, and create a positive cascading effect throughout the organization. Lamm, Tosti-Kharas, and King (2015) found employees who have sustainability inclinations behave sustainably; and have positive job attitudes, when they perceive their organizational culture supports, promotes, and encourages sustainability. Some organizational leaders even actively promote changing business mindsets to make decisions that are best for business and best for the environment, for the short- and long-term (Glavas & Mish, 2015). Individuals with strong economic values were more willing to work in ethically controversial industries; consequently, organizational leaders in those industries may have difficulty gaining their employee's support for corporate social or environmental issues (Marcus, MacDonald, & Sulsky, 2015). Lamm, Tosti-Kharas, and King (2015) contended psychological and structural empowerment is necessary to elicit positive organizational changes. Also, consider employee needs and perceptions, workflows, and compliance reporting, to establish a convenient procedure that makes sense (Gerard & Weber, 2015). Sustainability inclined employees in sustainability-oriented cultures tended to have higher job satisfaction and lower turnover, partly because they had opportunities to act (Lamm, Tosti-Kharas, & King, 2015). Even when given sufficient information, people that that did not have subject competence were more likely to take a conservative approach (Aren & Aydemir, 2015). By promoting values externally, organizational leaders work to establish a consistent definition of value in the market for consumers and suppliers through the implementation of standards,

certifications, and regulations (Glavas & Mish, 2015). However, forcing the

sustainability issue may not make financial sense at some point, and it may be time to

reevaluate sustainability initiatives (Lamm et al., 2015). Identity influences internal

stakeholders sense of who they are, and how they relate to external stakeholders (Morsing

& Roepstorff, 2015). Teaching acceptance of body-types, reducing accessibility to poor-

quality foods, and encouraging physical activity, may do more to promote healthy

lifestyle changes than weight-based programs alone (Penney & Kirk, 2015). However,

most ethical standards strengthening efforts will be quashed without consistent

implementation, congruency between managers and supervisors, or if leadership does not

exemplify the standards they established (Eisenbeiss et al., 2015). Zhang (2015)

adumbrated public attitudes and efforts may shape political and corporate actions

regarding the environment. Parashar (2015) reiterated the importance of the environment

by stating the natural environment is a prerequisite for life. However, the relevance of

sustainability is not a significant consideration for most people; so, there is a need to

improve discourse about the applicability of sustainability (Nambiar & Chitty, 2014).

Human constructions such as meaning, value, language, and imagination can be applied

to incorporate environmental considerations (Parashar, 2015). Cho (2015) augured

consumer demand often inspires moves toward sustainable organizational practices; and,

increased consumer knowledge about sustainability may shape consumer behavior.

Nijaki (2015) concluded there is not a prescriptive solution to achieve environmental

justice or sustainability, and progress in either area requires cognizance, discussion, and action. Colleagues, or third-party service companies, may be able to offer guidance or assessment tools to identify sustainability improvement opportunities (Ondrey, 2015).

Reputation. Journalists news reports of mendacious organizational leaders that make false sustainability claims can create backfire effects for the company and lead to negative market reactions (Du, 2015). Moog et al. (2015) found MSIs can help organizational leaders develop legitimacy; however, the legitimacy strategy is limited by the credibility of the participants in the MSI. When there is a negative image, internal stakeholders may become self-critical, and when there is a more positive perception than experienced, internal stakeholders may be inspired to improve (Morsing & Roepstorff, 2015). Du (2015) presupposed journalists' publications of claims, and actual results, can balance asymmetries. Morsing and Roepstorff (2015) recapitulated internal, and internal-external communications, fluidly make and re-make organizational identity. Public recognition of external accomplishments reinforces the internal culture that created the external recognition (Glavas & Mish, 2015).

Leadership. Leaders that do not inspire innovation in their organizations are managers (Sohmen, 2015). CEO leadership requires adeptness to satisfy the varying needs of internal and external stakeholders, respect for contextual influences, skill to negotiate unique internal and external dynamics, and projection (Eisenbeiss, van Knippenberg, & Fahrbach, 2015). Dynamic leaders proactively evaluate and introspect to determine the best positions and actions as they lead their teams to organizational advancement (Sohmen, 2015). Lampikoski et al. (2014) discussed proactive leaders move beyond regulatory compliance and work to capitalize on sustainable issues by aggregating internal and external resources. Sohmen (2015) says, leadership as a role, mindset, and set of behaviors, should diverge from the status quo practices that managers are hired to perform. Some business leaders boldly make sustainability requirements for their suppliers (Lampikoski, Westerlund, Rajala, & Möller, 2014). However, most CEOs rely on their executive staff for guidance on paths to take (Peters & Romi, 2015). Jacobson, Wasserman, Wu, and Lauer (2015) found presumptuous managers choose to control an organizational function that could be better managed if it were outsourced. Gore (2014) asserted hiring, or electing, a topic champion may aid in the advancement of some sustainability initiative. Outsourcing responsibilities can quickly fill specialization gaps with people better positioned to accomplish the tasks efficiently, allowing managers and team members to focus on core competencies (Jacobson, Wasserman, Wu, & Lauer, 2015). Leadership should steadfastly advance mutually beneficial relationships with trust and loyalty as foundations to reduce acquisition costs and improve reliability (Eisenbeiss et al., 2015). To improve their successfulness, leaders should employ creativity that attracts interest, competitiveness, and problem-solving utility to bring about innovation (Sohmen, 2015). Sohmen (2015) also asserted design thinking, creative problem solving, and system thinking, are other innovation tools for leaders.

Government. Lampikoski, Westerlund, Rajala, and Möller (2014) say environmental events and environmental legislation make sustainability an addressable topic. Morsing and Roepstorff (2015) contended organizational leaders move into the political sphere by pursuing environmental or social CSR objectives such as human rights, global warming, or deforestation. State, federal, national, and NGOs can be sources of income by aligning organizational objectives with State, Federal, National, and NGOs programs that offer discounts or other financial incentives (Jacobson et al., 2015). Organizational leaders can act apolitically; however, political topics still may be imposed on an organization (Morsing & Roepstorff, 2015). Fassin et al. (2015) reported, government can create CSR policy to influence awareness and relevance of CSR, sustainability, and stakeholder management. Mukherjee and Chakraborty (2013) identified increased political freedom, higher human development, and income growth, tend to be shared characteristics where there is environmental sustainability. Organizational leaders should consider their political involvement or stance especially in unstable or weak governments (Morsing & Roepstorff, 2015). Despite globalization, there are national differences in meanings of CSR and related concepts, so international business managers should be sensitive to local interpretations (Fassin et al., 2015).

Transition

Section 1 included the background of the problem, the problem and purpose statements, nature of the study, research and interview questions, and a discussion of the systems theory conceptual framework. Section 1 also included operational definitions, assumptions, limitations, and delimitations of this study, the significance of the study, and a review of relevant literature. The literature review was an explication of systems thinking and internal and external interdependencies. Systems thinking is the omnipresent concept that internal interdependencies and external interdependencies naturally reside in; so, internal and external interdependencies also began with a systems discourse. After systems thinking, there was an explication of how internal interdependencies relate to organizational sustainability and how managerial micro-decisions affect the macro-environment. Internal interdependencies consisted of five subsets: (1) systems (2) competition (3) financial (4) values and (5) reputation. Following internal systems, there was a discussion of external interdependencies, and how an external threat can foster internal opportunities. External interdependencies were developed through seven subsets: (1) systems (2) competition (3) financial (4) values (5) reputation (6) leadership and (7) government. Throughout the literature review there were discussions of previous research, synthesized findings, and compared and contrasted methods and findings to provide additional depth and breadth to the applicability of systems thinking in developing a business case for sustainability before incorporating sustainability. The literature concluded with a summary of section 1 key points before transitioning into Section 2. In section 2, there will be a deeper discussion of justifications for this study, researcher role, participants, and data collection and analysis procedures. Section 3 will be discussion, application for professional practice, and implications for social change.

Section 2: The Project

This single case study is about entrepreneurs that consciously consider systems from inception to execution. This study adds to the body of literature by describing the forethought of entrepreneurs that had the foresight to employ sustainable practices from the beginning of their business, rather than methodically transitioning to a system postulated to be more sustainable. Section 2 deliverables are purpose, researcher role, participants, a deeper discussion of method and design, population and sampling, ethical research, instruments, data collection and data organization techniques, data analysis, and reliability and validity.

Purpose Statement

The purpose of this qualitative single case study is to learn why international business managers have a business case for sustainability before they incorporate sustainability. The qualitative method and single case study design provide a rich context for exploration of one company in detail (Reynolds, 2014). The targeted population is a consulting firm comprised of 59 experienced international product development professionals based on the East Coast of the United States. The industry leaders of the private organization help entrepreneurs develop their natural products ideas at every phase from conception, to the retail outlet. Established in 2012, the natural products mavens have already fostered the development of 33 new brands. The consultants of the organization subscribe to the guiding principles of people-planet-profit-purpose as they serve their clients. The values-driven services the experts provide suggests the leaders understand why international business managers establish a business case for sustainability before they incorporate sustainability. Methods of inquiry include individual semi-structured interviews with 20 members of the leadership team (Reynolds, 2014). This study may yield new information that can benefit social change scholars and practitioners that desire to develop or improve their business case for sustainability knowledge, tactics, or strategy.

Role of the Researcher

People are the best data collection instruments for qualitative research because of the need to interview, observe, and analyze (Merriam, 2009). The aim of this research is to improve general business practices, not individual practice, as described in the Belmont Report (Belmont, 1979). The research will include brief voluntary interviews of adequately informed adults with no diminished autonomy that comprehend what this study is about (Belmont, 1979). One of the roles of this researcher is to select justly participants directly related to the study-problem, and work to maximize benefits without harming the participants (Belmont, 1979). Another role of this researcher is to interview participants to understand from their perspective what factors contribute to the decision process to establish a business case for sustainability before implementing sustainable elements (Reynolds, 2014). The interview protocol this researcher will follow is found in Appendix A (Reynolds, 2014). This researcher will ask the participants logical follow-up questions to clearly understand the research phenomenon from the perspective of the participants (Fassin et al., 2015). This researcher will casually monitor participant autonomy and will contact university committee members if participant autonomy changed during the interview (Belmont, 1979). After each interview, the researcher will synthesize each interviewee's responses to interview questions, and type a single paragraph response to each interview question for member checking. This research follows standard or accepted practices, and no part of this research is experimental, negating the need for preliminary safety and efficacy research to include a new procedure (Belmont, 1979).

This researcher has no personal connection to the subject company or any of its stakeholders. This researcher discovered the sustainably designed products of the subject company at a local grocery store. After learning more about the sustainably designed systems of the corporation, this researcher decided to explore the factors that contributed to their decision processes to establish a business case for sustainability before implementing sustainable elements. This researcher does have friends that live near the subject company, but the correlation is only coincidental. Empathetic to all things living; this researcher will refrain from imbuing personal worldviews into the study, and will listen to alternative points of view even if those views are in opposition to this researcher's personal worldview (Li & Lin, 2011). To reduce the risk of bias, this researcher will record answers and observations, review and rewrite notes for accuracy, reflect, and look for trends in the data (Reynolds, 2014).

Participants

Eligible participants for this study will have direct knowledge of factors that contribute to the decision process to establish a business case for sustainability before implementing sustainable elements (Reynolds, 2014; Holliday, 2010; Merriam, 2009). Participants are located at a firm on the East Coast of the United States. The firm is comprised exclusively of experienced professionals whose primary motivation is to help entrepreneurs develop and expand the business aspirations of the new entrepreneurs. The Founder, who is also the Chief Service Officer (CSO), established the company in 2012, and hand-picked his team of officers, directors, and advisors. The team of experts the Founder and CSO brought together has already introduced 33 new brands to the market. The people in those senior roles are the best choices for participants in this study because they are thought to have the highest level of knowledge, and should be able to answer the research questions (Merriam, 2009).

There are several strategies this researcher can use to gain access to the prospective participants. This researcher could request contact via their publicly available electronically submitted form, telephone number, fascimile, or direct mail address. This researcher will use all forms of publicly available contact information as needed, to request contact, and gain access to the Founder and CSO. The only anticipated gatekeeper for access to the Founder and CSO is a receptionist at the case study site. This researcher will build rapport with the Founder and CSO to facilitate connections with the purposively selected Chief Operations Officer, Chief Financial Officer, International Managing Director, and 16 of the 28 Advisors, to achieve adequate data saturation (Reynolds, 2014; Holliday, 2010; Amodeo, 2005). The strategies this researcher will use to build working relationships with interviewees during face-to-face individual interviews at the firm is to synergistically and actively engage, show interest through open dialog, be pleasant, positive, and respectful (Corcoran & McGuinness, 2014; Li & Murphy, 2013; Itolondo, 2013). Although this researcher is personable and professional; this researcher will kindly ask the Founder and CSO for introductions to the 19 other interviewees, because of the Founder and CSO's direct influence over the team (Reynolds, 2014; Holliday, 2010; Amodeo, 2005). This researcher will follow the directions of the Founder and CSO for initial contact with the 19 other interviewees. Initial contacts with the 19 other interviewees will include transmissions of the consent form for adults (see Appendix B) and the interview questions (see Appendix C).

Research Method and Design

Research Method

Business administration, as an applied social science, regularly involves the interaction of people (Merriam, 2009). A researcher's knowledge of a practice, and the desire to improve the practice, may lead to the study of the practice through a method (Merriam, 2009). The qualitative research method is a tool a researcher can use to understand the research subject from the perspective of the participants that regularly practice what the researcher desires to study (Reynolds, 2014). In that way, through researchable questions focused on discovery, insight can be gained for the benefit of the greater good (Merriam, 2009). Likewise, a human data collection instrument is best suited to derive meaning from context such as interviews, observation, and analysis as a basis for qualitative research (Wood, 2014). Thereby, a practical solution can be obtained to answer the research question that began the inquiry (Amodeo, 2005). Through systematic pure qualitative research, professionals may learn why international business managers have a business case for sustainability before they incorporate sustainability (Merriam, 2009).

Qualitative research questions follow the form of why and how (Wood, 2014). Although the body of knowledge regarding sustainability is growing, managers still do not have a clear understanding of the relevance of establishing a business case for sustainability before incorporating sustainability (Holiday, 2010). Additional contributions to the body of literature, from the perspective of entrepreneurs that understand why international business managers have a business case for sustainability before they incorporate sustainability, may help to improve the profitability of incorporating sustainable practices (Hinz, 2012).

Quantitative research is better suited to studies of well-known practices (Fassin et al., 2015). When subjects are well known, researchers can quantitatively determine to what extent an aspect is working (Merriam, 2009). Then, through qualitative research, researchers can incrementally improve the practice (Fassin et al., 2015; Merriam, 2009). Because of the lack of understanding of why international business managers have a business case for sustainability before they incorporate sustainability, a qualitative study at a firm where consciously considered systems to produce a sustainable effect provides a practical perspective of participants, and is a necessary contribution to the body of literature (Amodeo, 2005). Subsequently, managers seeking practical sustainability solutions may find information in this study that could apply to the firms they manage (Holiday, 2010).

Research Design

A research design should correlate with the research question, and should coincide with the worldview, personality, and skills of the researcher (Merriam, 2009).

The case study design is appropriate for the research questions in this study because the case study design will allow sharing and exploration of the breadth of experiences of the participants (Reynolds, 2014). This researcher's personality fits well with the case study design because this researcher's interview technique seems more like a naturally flowing conversation rather than an awkward introduction and interrogation. This researcher is not judgmental, and genuinely respects and appreciates individuals. Because the researcher will be comfortable, the participants should be comfortable to participate, and should respond to prompts freely. Conscientious sustainability frames this researcher's worldview. This researcher believes that properly applied systems thinking can improve productive efficiencies while simultaneously reducing negative externalities (Ardichvili, 2012). In this study, this researcher's worldview will aid this researcher in developing an understanding of why international business managers establish a business case for sustainability before the leaders incorporate sustainability.

Phenomenological, ethnographic, grounded theory, narrative analysis, and critical research are all inappropriate designs for this study. Phenomenology is about the essence of an experience (Merriam, 2009). The phenomenological design is ineffective in this study because the aim of this study is to explore the breadth of experiences that contribute to a business case for sustainability and not the essence of those experiences. Ethnographies involve investigation of social or cultural groups to find and describe beliefs, values, and attitudes that structure behavior, language, and interactions (Amodeo, 2005); the depth of thick description combined with the researcher's personal interpretation (Merriam, 2009), are out of the focus of this study. The aim of grounded theory is to build a theory or address processes that change over time (Merriam, 2009). Building a theory is inappropriate at present. Discussions at firms where systems, and the practical applications of systems to establish a business case for sustainability before incorporating sustainability, are not yet pervasive. This study will not benefit from attempting to address sustainability processes over time because sustainability processes are still in development, and not yet widespread (Holliday, 2010). A narrative analysis is a story as data, and is analyzed for the meaning it has for the author (Merriam, 2009). In a case study, the reader determines what applies to the reader's context (Merriam, 2009). The aim of critical research is to critique, challenge, transform, and empower (Merriam, 2009). Since sustainability is not well known or widely practiced, critical research is inappropriate to use at this time (Holliday, 2010). If sustainability becomes widely practiced, then critical research could contribute to improving sustainability practices.

This researcher will only interview participants that are thought to have the highest level of knowledge about developing a business case for sustainability before incorporating sustainability at the subject firm (Merriam, 2009). To ensure data saturation, reliability, and validity, this researcher will continue to interview participants at the subject firm until no new divulged information transpires and will seek approval of interview interpretations from the participants (Holliday, 2010). This researcher should be able to answer adequately all of the research questions in this study in less than 20 face-to-face individual interviews (Reynolds, 2014). However, to eliminate doubt that this researcher achieved saturation, this researcher will continue interviews until all 20 scheduled interviews are complete (Reynolds, 2014).

Population and Sampling

The targeted population is a consulting firm comprised of 59 experienced international product development professionals based on the East Coast of the United States. Each of the 59 professionals has a summary paragraph of their qualifications and accomplishments that justifies their current role in the subject company. After reviewing all of those experienced professional's summary paragraphs on the firm's website, this researcher will purposefully select 20 of the professionals to interview. The sampling purpose is to maximize information collected to answer the research questions, so the only interviews are of the experts, and not their subordinates (Merriam, 2009). External stakeholders or experts also will not be part of the sample. The purpose of this study is to understand why domestically-based international product development professionals, currently active in one company, develop a business case for sustainability before incorporating sustainability. The single case study design vividly allows this researcher to understand why leaders develop a business case before incorporating sustainability in the context of the process (Hinz, 2012).

Holiday (2010) purposefully interviewed senior executives, and was able to achieve saturation with only 12 participants in a single case study. Reynolds (2014) purposefully interviewed 20 managers, and was able to achieve saturation in a single case study. This researcher's single case study will include 20 individual interviews of accomplished people who hold senior positions. The senior roles include titles such as officer, director, and advisor. The senior members of the company have international business experience, entrepreneurial experience, or other similar product development leadership experience. The people in those senior roles are the best choices for

participants in this study because they are thought to have the highest level of knowledge,

and should be able to answer the research questions (Merriam, 2009). Interviews will

occur in a private meeting room at the subject company. The interview area will be free

from distractions, and quiet enough to prevent communication encumbrances. This

researcher will not wear cologne or other fragrances that could be distracting to

interviewees, but this researcher will wear business-casual attire to help make

interviewees feel comfortable. The interview will be around 45 minutes long, and the

researcher's language style will continue to be colloquial, while the questions will remain

formal. Interviews will take place before, during, or after business hours to accommodate

the interviewees.

This researcher will continue to interview participants at the subject firm until no

new information is divulged to ensure data saturation, reliability, and validity, (Reynolds,

2014; Holiday, 2010). After each interview, the researcher will synthesize each

interviewee's responses to interview questions, and type a single paragraph response to

each interview question for member checking. This researcher will seek approval from

each of the participants, and ask each participant if they want to add any information to

any of this researcher's interpretations of their responses (Holliday, 2010). The member

checking process will continue until participants divulge no new information.

Ethical Research

Participants in this study are not from protected classes. However, research

requires some disclosure and safeguarding of participant information. The consenting process is made formal with the consent form for adults (see Appendix B). The consent form begins with a written invitation for prospective participants to participate in the study, and introduces the researcher. Following the invitation and introduction are background information about why the subject is of interest a researcher, interview procedures that give prospective participants an overview of what to expect in the interview, and a few sample questions. The consent form also states that participation is voluntary, and participants will receive no compensation if they do choose to participate; but, their identity and the information they share will remain private (Holliday, 2010). The final doctoral manuscript will include the Walden University Internal Review Board (IRB) approval number (Reynolds, 2014).

If after reviewing the consent form for adults, prospective participant questions have been answered, and the prospective participant agrees to participate in the study, then the prospective participant and the researcher will sign the consent form for adults to formally agree to the terms of participation identified in the consent form (Reynolds, 2014). After the participant and the researcher have signed the consent form for adults, the researcher will give a signed copy of the form to the participant, that also has the researcher's contact information. During initial data collection, data transfer, and archiving, original hand-written and printed forms of data will be stored in the researcher's combination locked briefcase (Holliday, 2010). All digital iterations of study data will be kept secure in this researcher's password protected Dropbox except the digital voice recorder; the digital voice recorder will also be stored in the researcher's combination locked briefcase when it is not in use. No iteration of this study will include names or any other identifiable information of individuals or the subject organization; interview numbers are the only participant identification (Holliday, 2010). Data is secured for five years as required by Walden University to protect rights of participants (Reynolds, 2014). This researcher will delete digital data, and incinerate hand-written and printed documents after five years (Reynolds, 2014). Participant identification, and the name of the subject company, will remain hidden during and after the study. This researcher will know participant identification only to identify which participant's information to discard if the participant chooses not to participate in the study.

Participation in the study is voluntary so participants may withdraw from the study anytime, because an unwilling or uncooperative participant may compromise the integrity of the study (Hinz, 2012). A participant may discontinue participation without any repercussions by writing their request to discontinue participation on the specific consent form the participant originally used to give consent (Reynolds, 2014). If a participant withdraws, then data that was collected after informed consent and before discontinued informed consent, will be discarded. Then, this researcher will purposefully select another potential participant using the process described in the *population and sampling* subsection of this study (Fassin et al., 2015). This process to gain participants will continue until the 20th interview takes place.

Data Collection Instruments

This researcher will be the primary data collection instrument because of the need to interview, observe, and analyze (Merriam, 2009). Tools the researcher will use are an interview protocol (Appendix A), consent form for adults (Appendix B), questionnaire

(Appendix C), and digital voice recorder, to record participant responses. No instrument requires testing for reliability or validity because participants will not complete any instrument; therefore, concepts will necessitate neither measuring nor scoring. Instead, this researcher will collect raw data directly from the participants via semi-structured, focused interviews, in-person, and in the private meeting room at the subject company, so there will be little or no interruption (Reynolds, 2014). A person is the best data collecting instrument for a case study because a person can investigate and explore bounded systems using all available data collection techniques (Merriam, 2009). For instance, when participants give unexpected information, or when there are nuances in non-verbal communication, the individual researcher can identify and immediately react, adapt, or verify (Merriam, 2009). To maintain the fluidity of the interview process, data saturation, reliability and validity, this researcher will follow the simple sequential steps as described in the interview protocol (Appendix A) (Holliday, 2010). As per the interview protocol, this researcher will clarify background information of the study, procedures, sample questions, voluntary nature of the study, compensation, privacy, contact information, and statement of consent in the consent form for adults (Appendix B).

If the prospective participant agrees to be in this study, then the participant will sign the consent form for adults (Appendix B). Afterward, this researcher will ask the participant questions about factors that may go into the decision process to establish a business case for sustainability before incorporating sustainable elements (Appendix C). This researcher will have a blue ink pen to write participant responses on the pre-printed questionnaire, and this researcher will record the interview with a digital voice recorder. Later in the day, and not in the participant's presence, this researcher will review the recording and annotations, type the question, and type a one-paragraph synthesis of participant responses to each question. Then, this researcher will meet with each participant another time to seek approval of this researcher's interpretation of the participant's responses. This follow-up meeting will give the participant an opportunity to add, remove, or change any aspect of the researcher's interpretation of the participant's responses. This member checking process will continue until the participant approves this researcher's interpretation of the participant's responses with no changes necessary.

Data Collection Technique

Data collection will occur during participant interviews at site visits (Wood, 2014). This researcher will use a focused interview style to interview participants about their understanding of why international business managers have a business case for sustainability before they incorporate sustainability (Reynolds, 2014). Focused interviews are conversational in style; yet, the researcher still follows the design of the study by asking the open-ended questions described in (Appendix C) (Merriam, 2009). Interviews will take place before, during, or after business hours in order to accommodate interviewees. Each of the 20 interviews may take 45 minutes, and the researcher will only interview one participant per day. If an interview is interrupted, then this researcher will contact one of the other participants to check their availability and continue the interrupted interview on the next convenient day for the interviewee. If the interrupted interview is never completed, then this researcher will not use those results in this study.

After a completed interview, this researcher will go back to this researcher's hotel room, and start typing the interview questions while the interview is still fresh in this researcher's mind. After this researcher types the first interview question, this researcher will sequentially review the hand-written answers the researcher wrote during the interview. This researcher will objectively review participant responses to the interview questions to identify the ideas that answer the interview question (Holliday, 2010). As this researcher identifies the ideas that answer the interview questions, this researcher will type those answers underneath the typed question. For clarity, and the sake of thoroughly answering the question, this researcher will also review the digital voice recorder, and type any replies to the research question that this researcher may have missed in the original hand-written responses (Reynolds, 2014). After all hand-written and digital voice recorder answers have been reviewed and typed for the first interview question, this researcher will then retype the answers into one coherent paragraph. When the one-paragraph answer is complete to the best of this researcher's ability, this researcher will start the typed-answer process all over again with question 2, and continue the process until all seven interview questions have one-paragraph answers that flow and make sense.

For reliability and validity, this researcher will meet with the participant again at the participant's convenience for member checking (Holliday, 2010). The member checking process involves seeking approval of the researcher's interpretation of the participant's responses. This follow-up meeting will give the participant an opportunity to add, remove, or change any aspect of the researcher's interpretation of the participant's responses. This member checking process will continue until the participant approves this researcher's interpretation of the participant's responses with no changes necessary.

Advantages of the interview process are immediate answers to the interview questions, and the ability to follow-up for reliability and validity (Holliday, 2010). Interviewing participants at their work site is the best technique for this study because it will be the most efficient way to gather the most relevant data (Merriam, 2009). The interview questions, as the standardized data collection instrument, tie-in well with systems theory as the conceptual framework. A pilot study is not necessary because this researcher is present during the interview to clarify any interviewee questions as needed. Furthermore, the conceptual framework of systems theory fits well with the design of this study, so there is no requirement for a trial run.

Disadvantages of the interview process are risks of subjectivity and bias (Merriam, 2009). To prevent subjectivity and bias, this researcher will be cognizant of the line of inquiry described in the study, ask interview questions in an unbiased manner, maintain fluidity, and a conversational tone (Holliday, 2010). Another important consideration is the appearance of interviewee responses that may be too similar in nature (Yin, 2009). Interviewee responses that are too similar in nature could be the result of some conspiratorial agenda (Yin, 2009). If participants seem to behaving conspiratorially, then this researcher will note the similarities, complete the interview, call the committee chairperson for direction, and find other participants to interview at the subject company.

Data Organization Technique

Data will be collected from the participants at in-person interviews at the subject

location (Wood, 2014). With the participant's permission, this researcher will voice-

record each interview with a Samsung YP-U3 digital recording device. The digital

recording device generates a unique file number at the start of the recording; this

researcher will use that unique number as the interview number for the participant. This

researcher will write the unique interview number in the top right-hand corner of a pre-

printed sheet of paper that has all of the interview questions and room to write answers

(see Appendix A). During the interview, this researcher will annotate participant

responses in the area below the question, on the pre-printed question sheet. Hand-writing

participant responses during the interview provide a backup in-case the digital recording

device fails (Reynolds, 2014).

After the interview, and not in the participant's presence, this researcher will

review the voice recording and annotations, type the question in a Microsoft® Word

document, and type a one-paragraph synthesis of participant responses to each question

in this researcher's laptop computer. Each Microsoft® Word document will be coded

with the interview number as-given by the digital recording device. During initial data

collection, data transfer, and archiving, original hand-written and printed forms of data

will be stored in the researcher's combination locked briefcase (Holliday, 2010). All

digital iterations of study data will be kept secure in the researcher's password protected

Dropbox with the exception of the digital voice recorder; the digital voice recorder will

also be stored in the researcher's combination locked briefcase when it is not in use. No iteration of this study will include names or any other identifiable information of individuals or the subject organization; participants will only be identified by their interview number (Holliday, 2010). Data will be kept secure for five years as required by Walden University to protect rights of participants (Reynolds, 2014). After five years, digital data will be deleted and hand-written and printed documents will be incinerated (Reynolds, 2014).

Data Analysis

Qualitative research questions follow the form of why and how (Wood, 2014). Although the body of knowledge regarding sustainability is growing, managers still do not have a clear understanding of what factors contribute to the decision process to establish a business case for sustainability before implementing sustainable elements (Holiday, 2010). To find the answers to the research question, this researcher will collect data from multiple independent sources via semi-structured interviews at the subject company (Hinz, 2012). Seven interview questions, asked of 20 interviewees at the subject company, will enable this researcher to gather enough data necessary to triagulate the answers. Before the interview begins, this researcher and the interviewee will review and sign the consent form for adults (see Appendix B). Each data gathering interview will be around 45 minutes long, and this researcher will follow the interview protocol (see Appendix A). This researcher will have a blue ink pen to write participant responses on a pre-printed sheet of interview questions (see Appendix C) and this researcher will record the interview with a digital voice recorder. Later in the day, and not in the participant's presence, this researcher will review the recording and the hand-written answers to the interview questions (see Appendix E), type the question, and type a one-paragraph synthesis of participant responses to each question. Then, this researcher will meet with each study participant again to seek approval of this researcher's interpretation of the participant's responses. This follow-up meeting gives the participant an opportunity to add, remove, or change any aspect of this researcher's interpretation of interviewee responses. The member checking process continues until the interviewee approves this researcher's interpretation of replies with no changes necessary for reliability and validity. Interviewee approved typed answers to the interview questions are designated to be in Appendix F.

The interview questions (see Appendix C), in combination with the systems theory conceptual framework, allows this researcher to use effectively data triangulation to compare and validate participant responses (Amodeo, 2005). The systems thinking conceptual framework in combination with data triangulation enables this researcher to conceptualize connections, causes, and effects. The ability to see the interplay between a part of a system and a larger system is a skill that enables managers to see how their micro-organizational system connects with the macro-environmental system. This researcher will utilize systems thinking as the conceptual framework to identify the interconnectedness of participant responses, response interconnectivity with the organizational culture, and corporate culture interconnectivity with the natural environment, as an integral part of the process of data triangulating answers to the research question.

Reliability and Validity

Reliability

Case studies are a form of empirical social research, so the burden is on the researcher to ensure that the research product is reliable, dependable, confirmable, and is adequately data-saturated (Merriam, 2009). Multiple sources of evidence, a chain of evidence, and interviewee review and approval of a typed version of their responses ensures confirmability (Yin, 2009). Readers of this study will be able to identify clearly how this researcher drew conclusions from the chain of evidence. The chain of evidence begins with raw data collected from participants (see Appendix E), and ends with the interviewee approved typed answers to interview questions (see Appendix F). This researcher will be able to answer the research question after this researcher synthesizes the interviewee responses into typed one-paragraph answers, and the interviewee approves of those summations (Marshall & Rossman, 2011). To achieve confirmability, this researcher will present hand-written notes in Appendix E, and interviewee approved typed answers to the interview questions in Appendix F.

The objective of dependability is to ensure repeatability of the study process, and arrive at the same findings and conclusions (O'Reilly & Parker, 2013, Yin, 2009). This researcher achieves dependability in this study through member checking. Through member checking, participants have an opportunity to verify that the typed answers to the interview questions reflect the interviewee's thoughts. When a study is dependable, readers can confidently reference the study. The chain of evidence presented in this study enables readers to duplicate this researcher's research (Yin, 2009). To ensure dependability, data saturation, reliability, and validity, this researcher will continue to interview participants at the subject firm until no new information is divulged (Holliday, 2010).

Validity

Study creditability enables readers to believe study findings are in line with participant viewpoints. Since this researcher will not be involved in the decision process to develop a business case for sustainability before incorporating sustainability, this researcher is relying on the remembered experiences of the participants. Inference occurs when an event cannot be observed directly (Yin, 2009). To reduce the risks of misinformation from inference, this researcher will ask follow-up questions to delve deeper into the participant's memory of the experience (Fassin et al., 2015). This researcher will maintain creditability by earning the approval of interview interpretations from the participants through member checking (Holliday, 2010).

Researchers need to have a reference point to build-upon or refute. Transferability refers to the possibility a reader may choose to site this researcher's work to build on it or refute it in future research. The ability of business leaders to apply and transfer results or procedure to a study, or a real-world scenario, makes a study generalizable (Yin, 2009). The finished product of this study will be deemed generalizable, and could apply to business leaders and researchers even for out-of-context use (Yin, 2009). If the content of this study is used to solve a business problem, then the research objective was met (Graebner, Martin, & Roundy, 2012).

Transition and Summary

Section 2 delved deeper into the method and design of this study with the justification of design by building on the applied business problem statement and the nature of the study. The general business problem is international business leaders that implement sustainable practices without a clear business case may not profit from those initiatives. The specific business problem is international business managers do not establish a business case for sustainability before they incorporate sustainability. This study is qualitative in nature, and focused through the case study design. This researcher's role in the study is the data collection instrument. This researcher will collect data with a voice recorder, and in-writing, during face-to-face interviews. The member checking process is the tool this researcher uses to validate this researcher's interpretation of interviewee responses.

In section 3, results of participant interviews would have formed part of the report of findings. Answers to the research questions would have been in categories. I would have also discussed the implications of the study, application to professional practice, and recommendations for future studies. Of course, there is no section 3, because this research proposal was rejected.

This is the end of my proposal.

References

Abu, E. E., Ritchie, C., & Jones, E. (2012). Consulting the oracle? *International Journal of Contemporary Hospitality Management, 24*(6), 886-906. doi:10.1108/09596111211247227

Adu-Febiri, F. (2014). Educated for a world that does not exist: Issues in Africa's education and training programs. *Review of Human Factor Studies, 20*(1), 30-72. Available from http://search.proquest.com

Albrecht, P., & Greenwald, C. (2014). Financial materiality of sustainability. *Journal of Corporate Citizenship*, (56), 31-52. doi:10.9774/GLEAF.8757.2014.de.00003

Amodeo, R. A. (2005). *Becoming sustainable: Identity dynamics within transformational culture change at Interface* (Ph.D. dissertation). Available from ProQuest Dissertations & Theses database. (UMI No. 3180729).

Andrade, J. A. (2015). Reconceptualising whistleblowing in a complex world. *Journal of Business Ethics, 128*(2), 321-335. doi:http:10.1007/s10551-014-2105-z

Ardichvili, A. (2012). Sustainability or limitless expansion: Paradigm shift in HRD practice and teaching. *European Journal of Training and Development, 36*(9), 873-887. doi:10.1108/03090591211280946

Aren, S., & Aydemir, S. D. (2015). The moderation of financial literacy on the relationship between individual factors and risky investment intention. *International Business Research, 8*(6), 17-28. doi:10.5539/ibr.v8n6p17

Asiri, B. K. (2015). Investors' to reaction to marketing and financial announcements in the telecommunication sector. *Journal of Applied Finance and Banking, 5*(3), 123-143. Available from http://search.proquest.com

Bahar, V. S., Alam, K. M. S., Mahfuz, I., & Khar, T. (2015). Utilization of value stream analysis to implement redefined value: A social business perspective. *Review of Business & Finance Studies, 6*(2), 85-103. Available from http://search.proquest.com

Bai, C., & Sarkis, J. (2013). Green information technology strategic justification and evaluation. *Information Systems Frontiers, 15*(5), 831-847. doi:10.1007/s10796-013-9425-x

Bankston, Carl L., I., II. (2010). Social justice: Cultural origins of a perspective and a theory. *The Independent Review, 15*(2), 165-178. Available from http://search.proquest.com

Baudot, J. (2006). *Social justice in an open world: The role of the United Nations.* The International Forum for Social Development. Retrieved from http://www.un.org/esa/socdev/documents/ifsd/SocialJustice.pdf

Belmont. (1979, April 18). In United Sates Department of Health and Human Services The Belmont Report. Retrieved from http://www.hhs.gov/ohrp/humansubjects/guidance/belmont.html

Brandenburg, M., & Rebs, T. (2015). Sustainable supply chain management: A modeling perspective. *Annals of Operations Research, 229*(1), 213-252. doi:10.1007/s10479-015-1853-1

Brown, M. (2012). Speaking up for the natural landscape: A rhetorical dilemma. *Journal of Management and Sustainability, 2*(2), 96-111. doi:10.5539/jms.v2n2p96

Butler, T. A. (2004). *Leveraging sustainability: How companies enhance their eco-innovation success* (Ph.D dissertation). Available from ProQuest Dissertations and Theses database. (UMI No. 3157095).

Cai, F. (2015). How to tackle the slowdown of potential growth rate in china? *China Finance and Economic Review, 3*(1), 1-12. doi:10.1186/s40589-015-0009-4

Carson, S. G., Hagen, Ø., & Sethi, S. P. (2015). From implicit to explicit CSR in a Scandinavian context: The cases of HÅG and Hydro. *Journal of Business Ethics, 127*(1), 17-31. doi:10.1007/s10551-013-1791-2

Certified organic. (2010, February 16). In United States Department of Agriculture producers and handlers applying for organic certification. Retrieved from http://www.ams.usda.gov/AMSv1.0/ams.fetchTemplateData.do?template=TemplateN&navID=NationalOrganicProgram&leftNav=NationalOrganicProgram&page=NOPApplyingforOrganicCertification&description=Producers%20and%20Handlers%20Applying%20for%20Organic%20Certification&acct=nopgeninfo

Ciemleja, G., & Lace, N. (2011). The model of sustainable performance of small and medium-sized enterprise. *Engineering Economics, 22*(5), 501-509. doi:10.5755/j01.ee.22.5.968

Chassagnon, V. (2014). Toward a social ontology of the firm: Reconstitution, organizing entity, institution, social emergence and power. *Journal of Business Ethics, 124*(2), 197-208. doi:10.1007/s10551-013-1849-1

Cho, Y-N. (2015). Different shades of green consciousness: The interplay of sustainability labeling and environmental impact on product evaluations. *Journal of Business Ethics, 128*(1), 73-82. doi:10.1007/s10551-014-2080-4

Chuang, W-C., & Gober, P. (2015). Predicting hospitalization for heat-related illness at the census-tract level: Accuracy of a generic heat vulnerability index in Phoenix, Arizona (USA). *Environmental Health Perspectives (Online), 123*(6), 606. doi:10.1289/ehp.1307868

Corcoran, M., & McGuinness, C. (2014). Keeping ahead of the curve. *Library Management, 35*(3), 175-198. doi:10.1108/LM-06-2013-0048

Dean, J. (2014). Personal protective equipment: An antecedant to safe behavior? *Professional Safety, 59*(2), 41-46. Available from http://search.proquest.com

Du, X. (2015). How the market values greenwashing? Evidence from China. *Journal of Business Ethics, 128*(3), 547-574. doi:10.1007/s10551-014-2122-y

Eccles, R. G., & Serafeim, G. (2013). A Tale of Two Stories: Sustainability and the Quarterly Earnings Call. *Journal of Applied Corporate Finance, 25*(3), 8-19. doi:10.1111/jacf.12023

Eisenbeiss, S. A., van Knippenberg, D., & Fahrbach, C. M. (2015). Doing well by doing good? Analyzing the relationship between CEO ethical leadership and firm performance. *Journal of Business Ethics, 128*(3), 635-651. doi:10.1007/s10551-014-2124-9

Environmental justice. (2014, September 23). In United Sates Environmental Protection

    Agency what is environmental justice?. Retrieved from

    http://www.epa.gov/environmentaljustice/

Fassin, Y., Werner, A., Van Rossem, A., Signori, S., Garriga, E., von Weltzien Hoivik,

    H., & Schlierer, H.-J. (2015). CSR and related terms in SME owner-managers'

    mental models in six European countries: National context matters. *Journal of*

    Business Ethics, 128(2), 433-456. doi:10.1007/s10551-014-2098-7

Frerichs, L., Brittin, J., Sorensen, D., Trowbridge, M. J., Yaroch, A. L., Siahpush, M.,

    Tibbits, M., & Huang, T. T.-K. (2015). Influence of school architecture and

    design on healthy eating: A review of the evidence. *American Journal of Public*

    Health, 105(4), E46-E57. doi:10.2105/ajph.2014.302453

Gerard, J. A., & Weber, C. M. (2015). Compliance and corporate governance:

    Theoretical analysis of the effectiveness of compliance based on locus of

    functional responsibility. *International Journal of Global Business, 8*(1), 15-26.

    Available from http://search.proquest.com

Glavas, A., & Mish, J. (2015). Resources and capabilities of triple bottom line firms:

    Going over old or breaking new ground? *Journal of Business Ethics, 127*(3), 623-

    642. doi:10.1007/s10551-014-2067-1

Gore, T. (2014). The role of policy champions and learning in implementing horizontal

    environmental policy integration: Comparative insights from European structural

    fund programmes in the U.K. *Administrative Sciences 4*(3), 304-330.

    doi:10.3390/admsci4030304

Graebner, M. E., Martin, J. A., & Roundy, P. T. (2012). Qualitative data: Cooking

without a recipe. *Strategic Organization, 10*(3), 276-284.

doi:10.1177/1476127012452821

Guerci, M., Radaelli, G., Siletti, E., Cirella, S., & Rami Shani, A. B. (2015). The impact

of human resource management practices and corporate sustainability on

organizational ethical climates: An employee perspective. *Journal of Business*

Ethics, 126(2), 325-342. doi:10.1007/s10551-013-1946-1

Hahn, T., Pinkse, J., Preuss, L., & Figge, F. (2015). Tensions in corporate sustainability:

Towards an integrative framework. *Journal of Business Ethics, 127*(2), 297-316.

doi:10.1007/s10551-014-2047-5

Hinz, A. (2012). *Knowledge management as a requirement for successful sustainability*

management (Doctoral dissertation). Available from EBSCO Host Business

Source Complete Dissertation database. (Accession No. 91913250).

Holliday, S. (2010). *A case study of how DuPont reduced its environment footprint: The*

role of organizational change in sustainability (Ed.D. dissertation). Available

from ProQuest Dissertations & Theses database. (UMI No. 3397435).

Itolondo, W. A. (2013). Teacher improvement through peer teacher evaluation in kenyan

schools. *European Journal of Training and Development, 37*(7), 635-645.

doi:10.1108/EJTD-10-2012-0047

Jacobson, P. D., Wasserman, J., Wu, H. W., & Lauer, J. R., (2015). Assessing

entrepreneurship in governmental public health. *American Journal of Public*

Health, 105, S318-S322. doi:10.2105/ajph.2014.302388

James, M. L. (2013). Sustainability and integrated reporting: Opportunities and

strategies for small and midsize companies. *Entrepreneurial Executive, 18*, 17-

28. Available from http://search.proquest.com

Jesper, K. J., Kristin, B. M., & Arlbjørn, J. S. (2013). Chasing value offerings through

green supply chain innovation. *European Business Review, 25*(2), 124-146.

doi:http://dx.doi.org/10.1108/09555341311302657

Johnson, D. B. (1996). *Four comparative case studies of socioecological responsibility:*

Organizational paradigms and environmental outcomes within the agroecological

business system (Ph.D. dissertation). Available from ProQuest Dissertations and

Theses database. (UMI No. 9632902).

Kiron, D., Kruschwitz, N., Reeves, M., & Goh, E. (2013). The benefits of sustainability-

driven innovation. *MIT Sloan Management Review, 54*(2), 69-73. Available

from http://search.proquest.com

Kotecha, P., Diwekar, U., & Cabezas, H. (2013). Model-based approach to study the

impact of biofuels on the sustainability of an ecological system. *Clean*

Technologies and Environmental Policy, 15(1), 21-33.

doi:10.1007/s10098-012-0491-4

Lamm, E., Tosti-Kharas, J., & King, C. (2015). Empowering Employee Sustainability:

Perceived organizational support toward the environment. *Journal of Business*

Ethics, 128(1), 207-220. doi:10.1007/s10551-014-2093-z

Lampikoski, T., Westerlund, M., Rajala, R., & Möller, K. (2014). Green Innovation

Games: Value-creation strategies for corporate sustainability. *California*

Management Review, 57(1), 88-116. doi:10.1525/cmr.2014.57.1.88

LEED. (2014). In United States Green Building Council LEED. Retrieved from http://www.usgbc.org/leed

Li, M., & Lin, K. (2011). A new paradigm of organizational transformation: Enacting wholeness praxis in the oneness of problem and possibility. *Systemic Practice & Action Research, 24*(2), 107-132. doi:10.1007/s11213-010-9179-z

Li, N., & Murphy, W. H. (2013). Consumers' alliance encounter satisfaction, attributions, and behavioral intentions. *The Journal of Consumer Marketing, 30*(6), 517-529. doi:10.1108/JCM-06-2013-0601

Lopatta, K., & Kaspereit, T. (2014). The world capital markets' perception of sustainability and the impact of the financial crisis. *Journal of Business Ethics, 122*(3), 475-500. doi:10.1007/s10551-013-1760-9

Lu, C., & Chueh, T. (2015). Corporate social responsibility and information asymmetry. *Journal of Applied Finance and Banking, 5*(3), 105-122.

Maclean, T., Litzky, B. E., & Holderness, D. K. (2015). When organizations don't walk their talk: A cross-level examination of how decoupling formal ethics programs affects organizational members. *Journal of Business Ethics, 128*(2), 351-368. doi:10.1007/s10551-014-2103-1

Maletic, M., Maletic, D., Dahlgaard, J. J., Dahlgaard-Park, S., & Gomiscek, B. (2014). The relationship between sustainability-oriented innovation practices and organizational performance: Empirical evidence from Slovenian organizations. *Organizacija, 47*(1), 3-13. doi:10.2478/orga-2014-0001

Malhotra, A., Melville, N. P., & Watson, R. T. (2013). Spurring impactful research on information systems for environmental sustainability. *MIS Quarterly, 37*(4), 1265-1274. Available from http://search.ebscohost.com

Marcus, J., MacDonald, H. A., & Sulsky, L. M. (2015). Do personal values influence the propensity for sustainability actions? A policy-capturing study. *Journal of Business Ethics, 127*(2), 459-478. doi:10.1007/s10551-013-2032-4

Mariappanadar, S. (2012). The harm indicators of negative externality of efficiency focused organizational practices. *International Journal of Social Economics, 39*(3), 209-220. doi:10.1108/03068291211199378

Marshall, C., & Rossman, G. (5th ed.). (2011). *Designing Qualitative Research.* Thousand Oaks, CA: Sage.

Mbah, S. E., & Ifeanyi, I. I. (2012). Consensus building: Implications for labour - management relations in Nigeria. *Journal of Management and Sustainability, 2*(1), 190-199. doi:10.5539/jms.v2n1p190

Mehalik, M. M. (2001). *System analysis of an environmentally sustainable textile system* (Ph.D. dissertation). Available from ProQuest Dissertations and Theses database. (UMI No. 3022115).

Merriam, S. B. (2009). *Qualitative research: A guide to design and implementation.* San Francisco, CA: Jossey-Bass.

Moog, S., Spicer, A., & Böhm, S. (2015). The politics of multi-stakeholder initiatives: The crisis of the forest stewardship council. *Journal of Business Ethics, 128*(3), 469-493. doi:10.1007/s10551-013-2033-3

Morsing, M., & Roepstorff, A. (2015). CSR as corporate political activity: Observations on IKEA's CSR identity-image dynamics. *Journal of Business Ethics, 128*(2), 395-409. doi:10.1007/s10551-014-2091-1

Mukherjee, S., & Chakraborty, D. (2013). Is environmental sustainability influenced by socioeconomic and sociopolitical factors? Cross-country empirical evidence. *Sustainable Development, 21*(6), 353-371. doi:10.1002/sd.502

Nambiar, P., & Chitty, N. (2014). Meaning making by managers: Corporate discourse on environment and sustainability in India. *Journal of Business Ethics, 123*(3), 493-511. doi:10.1007/s10551-013-1848-2

Nijaki, L. K. (2015). Justifying and juxtaposing environmental justice and sustainability: Towards an inter-generational and intra-generational analysis of environmental equity in public administration. *Public Administration Quarterly, 39*(1), 85-116. Available from EBSCO Host Business Source Complete database. (Accession No. 102300227.).

Ondrey, G. (2015). Flame retardants: Safety is the key. *Chemical Engineering, 122*(6), 19-23. Available from http://search.proquest.com

O'Reilly, M., & Parker, N. (2013). 'Unsatisfactory Saturation': A critical exploration of the notion of saturated sample sizes in qualitative research. *Qualitative Research 13*(2), 190-197. doi:10.1177/1468794112446106

Organic. (2014, December 12). In United Sates Department of Agriculture what is organic?. Retrieved from http://www.ams.usda.gov/AMSv1.0/nop

Panwar, R., Paul, K., Nybakk, E., Hansen, E., & Thompson, D. (2014). The legitimacy of CSR actions of publicly traded companies versus family-owned companies. *Journal of Business Ethics, 125*(3), 481-496. doi:10.1007/s10551-013-1933-6

Parashar, A. (2015). Reverberations of environmental crisis and its relevance in managing sustainability: An ecocritical reading of T. S. Eliot's The Waste Land. *Decision, 42*(2), 159-172. doi:10.1007/s40622-015-0081-5

Penney, T. L., & Kirk, S. F. L. (2015). The health at every size paradigm and obesity: Missing empirical evidence may help push the reframing obesity debate forward. *American Journal of Public Health, 105*(5), E38-E42. doi:10.2105/ajph.2015.302552

Perez-Vega, S., Ortega-Rivas, E., Salmeron-Ochoa, I., & Sharratt, P. N. (2013). A system view of solvent selection in the pharmaceutical industry: Towards a sustainable choice. *Environment, Development and Sustainability, 15*(1), 1-21. doi:10.1007/s10668-012-9365-5

Peters, G. F., & Romi, A. M. (2015). The association between sustainability governance characteristics and the assurance of corporate sustainability reports. *Auditing: A Journal of Practice & Theory, 34*(1), 163-198. doi:10.2308/ajpt-50849

Ping, C. (2014). The application of system analysis methods in the study of corporate social responsibility system. *International Journal of Business and Social Science, 5*(10), 272-280. Available from http://search.proquest.com

Prust, M. L., Clark, K., Davis, B., Pallas, S. W., Kertanis, J., O'Keefe, E., Araas, M., Lyer, N. S., Dandorf, S., Platis, S., Humphries, D., (2015). How Connecticut health directors deal with public health budget cuts at the local level. *American*

Journal of Public Health, 105,(S2), S268-S273. doi:10.2105/ajph.2014.302499

Reale, E. (2014). Challenges in higher education research: The use of quantitative tools in comparative analyses. *Higher Education, 67*(4), 409-422. doi:10.1007/s10734-013-9680-2

Reynolds, H. (2014). *Organizational ambidexterity at a department level* (Doctoral dissertation). Available from ProQuest Dissertations & Theses database. (UMI No. 3611500).

Robinson, S. (2015). Islam, responsibility and business in the thought of Fethullah Gülen. *Journal of Business Ethics, 128*(2), 369-381. doi:10.1007/s10551-014-2101-3

Roulet, T. J., & Touboul, S. (2015). The intentions with which the road is paved: Attitudes to liberalism as determinants of greenwashing. *Journal of Business Ethics, 128*(2), 305-320. doi:http:10.1007/s10551-014-2097-8

Rueede, D., & Kreutzer, K. (2015). Legitimation work within a cross-sector social partnership. *Journal of Business Ethics, 128*(1), 39-58. doi:10.1007/s10551-014-2072-4

Sehu, E., & Dobric, D. (2014). University-employer cooperation. *Beijing Law Review, 5*(4), 272-282. doi:10.4236/blr.2014.54026

Shaheen, S. A., & Bansal, A. (2015). Perceptions of peer-to-peer carsharing in the San Francisco bay area, CA, USA. *Institute of Transportation Engineers. ITE Journal, 85*(5), 39-42. Available from http://search.proquest.com

Shen, C. (2014). The result of systems thinking as knowledge assets work in an organization. *Journal of International Management Studies, 9*(2), 95-104.

Available from http://search.proquest.com

Shuv-Ami, A. (2013). Social protest: The Israeli case. *Journal of Enterprising Communities, 7*(4), 373-382. doi:10.1108/JEC-06-2012-0039

Sohmen, V. S. (2015). Reflections on creative leadership. *International Journal of Global Business, 8*(1), 1-14. Available from http://search.proquest.com

Storsletten, V. M., L., & Jakobsen, O. D. (2015). Development of leadership theory in the perspective of Kierkegaard's philosophy. *Journal of Business Ethics, 128*(2), 337-349. doi:10.1007/s10551-014-2106-y

Swaim, J. A., Maloni, M. J., Napshin, S. A., & Henley, A. B. (2014). Influences on student intention and behavior toward environmental sustainability. *Journal of Business Ethics, 124*(3), 465-484. doi:10.1007/s10551-013-1883-z

Von Bertalanffy, L., (1972). The history and status of general systems theory. *Academy of Management Journal, 15*(4), 407-426. doi:10.2307/255139

Wexler, L., Chandler, M., Gone, J. P., Cwik, M., Kirmayer, L. J., LaFromboise, T., Brockie, T., O'Keefe, V., Walkup, J., Allen, J. (2015). Advancing suicide prevention research with rural American Indian and Alaska native populations. *American Journal of Public Health, 105*(5), 891-899. doi:10.2105/ajph.2014.302517

Wolfgramm, R., Flynn-Colemann, S., & Conroy, D. (2015). Dynamic interactions of agency in leadership (DIAL): An integrative framework for analysing agency in sustainability leadership. *Journal of Business Ethics 126*(4), 649-662.

doi:10.1007/s10551-013-1977-7

Wood, M. W. (2014). *Addressing sustainability in an entrepreneurship ecosystem: A case study of a social incubator in Mexico* (Doctoral dissertation). Available from ProQuest Dissertations & Theses database. (UMI No. 3619598).

Yin, R. K. (4th ed.) (2009). *Case study research: Design and methods.* Thousand Oaks, CA: Sage.

Zeidan, R., Boechat, C., & Fleury, A. (2015). Developing a sustainability credit score system. *Journal of Business Ethics, 127*(2), 283-296. doi:10.1007/s10551-013-2034-2

Zeng, Y. (2014). Research on enterprise strategic reconstruction and path selection based on institutional change. *International Journal of Business and Social Science, 5*(6), 304-310. Available from http://search.proquest.com

Zhang, Y. (2015). The regulatory framework and sustainable development of China's electricity sector. *The China Quarterly, 222*, 475-498. doi:10.1017/S0305741015000727

Zhang, W., & Zhang, Q. (2014). Multi-stage evaluation and selection in the formation process of complex creative solution. *Quality and Quantity, 48*(5), 2375-2404. doi:10.1007/s11135-013-9896-3

Appendix A: Interview Protocol

Participant: _____ Interview Number: _____

Instructions:

- Casually reintroduce each other, and then give a brief overview to the participant of the purpose of the study.

- Assure confidentiality and have the participant sign the consent form for adults.

- Use a digital voice recorder to record interview audio and assign a chronological interview number as given by the digital voice recorder.

- Record chronological participant interview number on top of the page next to the participant's name.

- Ask the participant questions in-order, and ask relevant follow-up questions for clarity and deep understanding, naturally in a conversational tone.

- Record responses in the spaces below each printed question.

- Thank the participant for their participation.

- Review interviewee responses and the digital voice recording of the interview.

- Type each question and a one paragraph answer as described by the participant.

- Provide a printed copy of the typed questions and one-paragraph interpreted answers to the participant for review.

- Ask the participant if the interpreted answers accurately represent the participant's intentions and if any information should be added, removed, or changed.

- Continue the member checking process until no changes are necessary.

- Thank the participant for their participation.

Appendix B: Consent Form for Adults

You are invited to voluntarily participate in research about developing a business case for sustainability before incorporating sustainable elements. The researcher is inviting the Founder and Chief Service Officer, Chief Operations Officer, Chief Financial Officer, International Managing Director, and 16 of the 28 Advisors to be in this study. This form is part of a process called "informed consent" to allow you to understand this study before deciding whether to take part.

This research is being conducted by a researcher named Richard Holzmuller, who is a doctoral student at Walden University. Richard Holzmuller has no connection to anyone associated with this company or any other company that could be considered a direct or indirect competitor to the subject firm so there is no potential conflict of interest.

Background Information:

The purpose of this study is to learn why international business managers establish a business case for sustainability before they incorporate sustainability. Sustainability is conservation, deployment, and reuse of resources in responsible ways. There has been a lot of research about practices at companies that transition their companies to include sustainable practices, but there have not been any studies about the systems considerations business leaders have when they develop a business case for sustainability before incorporating sustainable elements.

Procedures:
If you agree to be in this study, you will be asked to answer questions about factors that may go into the decision process to establish a business case for sustainability before incorporating sustainable elements. The interview will be around 45 minutes long. The researcher will have a blue ink pen to write your responses on the pre-printed questionnaire, and the researcher will record the interview with a digital voice recorder. Later in the day, and not in your presence, the researcher will review the recording and his annotations, type the question, and type a one-paragraph synthesis of your responses to each question. Then, the researcher will meet with you again to seek your approval of the researcher's interpretation of your responses. This follow-up meeting will give you an opportunity to add, remove, or change any aspect of the researcher's interpretation of your responses. This member checking process will continue until you approve the researcher's interpretation of your responses with no changes necessary.

Here are some sample questions:

Why do not international business managers establish a business case for sustainability before they incorporate sustainability?
How do internal factors contribute to the decision process to establish a business case for sustainability before implementing sustainable features?

How do not external factors contribute to the decision process to set up a business case for sustainability before implementing sustainable features?
Why or how would anything else influence processes international business managers use to develop a business case for sustainability before implementing sustainable features?

Voluntary Nature of the Study:
Being in this study involves some risk of the minor discomforts that can be encountered in daily life such as the feeling of being inconvenienced or the feeling of stress from being inconvenienced. Being in this study will not pose risk to your safety or wellbeing. If you choose to participate, and later choose to not participate, there will not be any penalty to you, the researcher, or the University.

The benefit of participating in this study is that your contribution may help organizational leaders make decisions regarding tactics and strategies for developing a business case for sustainability before incorporating sustainable elements. Ideally, their choices will bring about positive change for their organization, employees, customers, and the environment.

Payment:
There is no payment, compensation, or other inducement for your participation in this study. Also, there will be no thank you gift.

Privacy:
Any information you provide will be kept confidential. The researcher will not use your personal information for any purposes outside of this research project. Also, the researcher will not include your name or anything else that could identify you in study reports. During initial data collection, data transfer, and archiving, original hand-written and printed forms of data will be stored in the researcher's combination locked briefcase. All digital iterations of study data will be kept secure in the researcher's password protected Dropbox with the exception of the digital voice recorder; the digital voice recorder will also be stored in the researcher's combination locked briefcase when it is not in use. Data will be kept for five years as required by Walden University. After five years, digital data will be deleted and hand-written and printed documents will be incinerated.

Contacts and Questions:
You may ask any questions you may have now. Or if you have questions later, you may contact the researcher via cell/text: 605-x90-19xx or via email: richard.holzmuller10@waldenu.edu. If you want to talk privately about your rights, as a participant, you can call Dr. x x. She is the Walden University representative who can discuss this with you. Her phone number is 1-800-925-3368, extension xx10. Walden University's approval number for this study is XXX and it expires on XXX.

The researcher will give you a copy of this form to keep.

Statement of Consent:
I have read the above information and I feel I understand the study well enough to make a decision about my involvement. By signing below, I understand that I am agreeing to the terms described above.

Printed Name of Participant   _____

Participant's Signature   _____

Date of Consent   _____

Researcher's Printed   _____

Researcher's Signature   _____

Appendix C: Interview Questions

1. Why do not international business managers establish a business case for
    sustainability before they incorporate sustainability?

2. Why do international business managers develop a business case for sustainability
    before they incorporate sustainability?

3. How do not internal factors contribute to the decision process to develop a business
    case for sustainability before implementing sustainable elements?

4. How do internal factors contribute to the decision process to establish a business case
    for sustainability before implementing sustainable features?

5. How do not external factors contribute to the decision process to set up a business
    case for sustainability before implementing sustainable features?

6. How do external factors contribute to the decision process to establish a business case
    for sustainability before implementing sustainable elements?

7. Why or how would anything else influence processes international business managers
    use to develop a business case for sustainability before implementing sustainable
    features?

Curriculum Vitae

Richard Holzmuller, M.B.A.

Lease Operator, *Petroleum Production Co.*

Doctoral candidate, *Walden University*

December 26, 2015

12xx Quincy St

Rapid City, SD 57701

(*mobile*) 605-x90-19xx

prestigeproper.com

Research Overview

Currently I am editing my doctoral study proposal. My doctoral study will be a case study on a company in the United States to learn why international business managers develop a business case for sustainability before incorporating sustainability. The aim of the study is to identify what systems considerations leaders have as they develop a business case for sustainability before incorporating sustainable elements. Entrepreneurs, organizational leaders at existing firms, and the people they serve, may benefit from the research when they apply what they learn from those leading edge sustainability innovators.

Education

Walden University 2009-2015

Doctor of Business Administration—All but Dissertation (A.B.D.)

National American University 2007-2009

Master of Business Administration, September 2009

National American University 2005-2006

Bachelor of Science Applied Management, November 2006

Davenport University 2003-2004

Marketing Major

Santa Fe Community College, 2002

Information Technology Major

Community College of the Air Force 1997-2001

Associate of Applied Science Avionic Systems, Spring 2001

Professional Activities

Ritchie Nordstrom for City Council, 2011 & 2013

Committee Member and Marketing Materials Development

Rapid City Chamber of Commerce, 2011-2012

Ambassador Committee Member

Committee to Elect Mathew Murray District 32 House of Representatives, 2010

Campaign Co-Chairperson

Breadroot Food Cooperative, 2010-2012

Board of Directors Secretary

Cathedral of Our Lady of Perpetual Help, 2005-2012

Espiritus Choir Member

Work Experience

Multiple Skilled Operator—Petroleum Production Companies, April 2013-present

Manage, and visit daily, 46 wells on a route

Ensure wells are producing oil and trouble-shoot wells that are down

Sell oil, prepare oil tanks for sale, and order production water disposal

Minor mechanical maintenance of production equipment

Collect production data at leases, data entry, and daily reports

Regular communication with supervisors, engineers, production assistants, etc. of well status

Safety meetings every other week and daily safety observations

Real Estate Owner/Broker—Licensed in SD and PA, January 2004-December 2012

LLC business development and management including revenues, disbursements, and sales tax

Marketing management from inception to execution for digital and print advertising

Business-to-Business and Person-to-Person networking

Social media marketing content origination

Manage accounts receivable/payable

Track current rentals, tenants, expenses, and provide year end client summaries

Balance checking and trust accounts

Parenting Specialist—Wellspring October 2011-December 2012

Supervise by setting limits, enforcing standards, giving praise, and holding accountable.

Residential Life Specialist—Sky Ranch for Boys September 2007-December 2009

Supervise by setting limits, enforcing standards, giving praise, and holding accountable.

Organize activities, document, and lead groups for the productive development of students.

Front Desk Clerk—Villager Lodge, FL; Durst Enterprises, SD July 2002-November 2004

Provide customer service over-the-phone or in-person

Follow-up scheduled departures to help facilitate housekeeping planning

Assistant Manager—Long John Silver's & David's Real Pit BBQ September 2001-July 2002

Manage three to six employees on a daily basis with write-ups and praise as needed

Measure daily inventories. Cross-reference with usage reports. Calculate variance

Verify employee work completed accurately. Track employee hours in log book

Resolve customer complaints. Reconcile daily transactions with quotas-reports

Avionics Test Station Journeyman—United States Air Force August 1997-July 2001

Troubleshoot electronics to component level via diagnostic programs, and technical orders

Perform regular preventative maintenance on test stations to help reduce equipment downtime

Procure mission essential assets by utilizing developed relationships of outside organizations

Trained and orientated new teammates to perform essential shop procedures

Honors and Awards

City of Rapid City Mayor Alan Hanks 2011

Certificate of Recognition and Appreciation

Coldwell Banker Lewis-Kirkeby-Hall 2005

Exceptional Customer Service Award

Ellsworth Air Force Base 28th Maintenance Squadron 1999

Airman of the Year

Ellsworth Air Force Base 28th Maintenance Squadron 1999

Airman of the Quarter

Ellsworth Air Force Base 28th Maintenance Squadron 1999

Maintenance Professional of the Month

Additional Achievements

Swimming 2010

Swam in the Pacific Ocean on a Wednesday and the Atlantic Ocean that Saturday

Running 2010

Macedonia, Istanbul, Mackinac Island, Central Park, Hermosa and Manhattan Beaches

Selected Media

Rapid City Journal 2011

Photographed and interviewed about property management in Rapid City, SD

Rapid City Journal 2010

Photographed while campaigning for Mathew Murray

Interests

Boating

Recreational

Documentaries

Social and cultural

Leisure Travel

Domestic and international

Blogging

Electronic & other independent music, diet & exercise, sustainability

www.ingramcontent.com/pod-product-compliance
Lightning Source LLC
Chambersburg PA
CBHW080945170526
45158CB00008B/2385